The ACT Approach

The ACT Approach

The Use of Suggestion for Integrative Learning

Expanded Second Edition

Lynn Dhority
University of Massachusetts
Boston, USA

Gordon and Breach Science Publishers
USA Switzerland Australia Belgium France Germany Great Britain
India Japan Malaysia Netherlands Russia Singapore

Second Printing published 1992 under license by Gordon and Breach Science Publishers S.A.

Gordon and Breach Science Publishers

5301 Tacony Street, Drawer 330
Philadelphia, Pennsylvania 19137
United States of America

Glinkastrasse 13-15
O-1086 Berlin
Germany

Y-Parc
Chemin de la Sallaz
CH-1400 Yverdon, Switzerland

Post Office Box 90
Reading, Berkshire RG1 8JL
Great Britain

Private Bag 8
Camberwell, Victoria 3124
Australia

3-14-9, Okubo
Shinjuku-ku, Tokyo 169
Japan

58, rue Lhomond
75005 Paris
France

Emmaplein 5
1075 AW Amsterdam
Netherlands

First available in manuscript form in 1984 as *Acquisition through Creative Teaching: ACT* by the Center for Continuing Development, Sharon, Massachusetts, USA.

Expanded Second Edition published in 1991 as *The ACT Approach: The Artful Use of Suggestion for Integrative Learning* by PLS Verlag GmbH, Bremen, West Germany.

Mindmap illustrations by Dan Gee.

Library of Congress Cataloging-in-Publication Data

Dhority, Lynn, 1939-
    The ACT Approach : the use of suggestion for integrative learning
  / Lynn Dhority. — 2nd expanded ed.
      p. cm.
  Rev. ed. of: Acquisition through creative teaching / Center for
Continuing Development. 1984.
  Includes bibliographical references (p.).
  ISBN 2-88124-553-6. -- ISBN 2-88124-556-0 (pbk.)
  1. Learning, Psychology of. 2. Mental suggestion. 3. Language
and languages--Study and teaching--Psychological aspects.
  I. Acquisition through creative teaching. II. Title.
LB1069.D47   1992
370.15'23--dc20   92-15712
                                                   CIP

Dedicated to Rosalind
who with great heartwarmth and mental clarity
provided sustaining support and guidance

CONTENTS

PREFACE

This edition represents a thorough reworking, expansion and updating of an earlier work, distributed in manuscript form under the title *Acquisition through Creative Teaching (ACT)*.

This book is written for teachers, that is, for a wide range of professional communicators and facilitators of learning. Its theme is how we as teachers can more consciously and effectively use the extraordinary dimensions and qualities we all possess—and in the process profoundly influence the learning experience of our students. It explores the remarkable phenomenon of suggestion, an aspect of our reality which we normally use with little awareness, and how, when we use it purposefully and consciously, it can become a powerful tool to enhance our teaching experiences and the learning experiences of our students.

The book is designed to serve several purposes:

- To provide a practical guide for teachers who wish to learn how to use the art of suggestion to help students tap remarkable brain capacities.

- To offer a comprehensive description of the suggestive learning process.

- To offer documentation of classroom results which establish persuasive arguments for the superiority of methods which focus on the learning process at both subconscious and conscious levels.

- And, specifically for second language teachers, to offer a model for second language acquisition which has proven itself to be effective, lively and fun—for both the teacher and the student.

The ACT Approach seeks to provide a holistic—whole-brain, whole-person—model for learning. Here, it is presented as a model for the teaching and acquisition of foreign languages, but it can be adapted for teaching and learning nearly anything.[1] At one level it rests on my own twenty years experience in the classroom as a teacher of language, literature and psychology. More significantly, I believe, it has evolved from research outside foreign language methodology proper—specifically, out of investigations into how students learn best and how we as teachers can best facilitate the learning process.

Four influences have contributed most to the evolution of the ACT Approach:

- The holistic models of human development offered by Carl Jung and Roberto Assagioli. Psychosynthesis, developed by Assagioli, provided both practical psychological and spiritual cornerstones for a holistic model of learning and teaching.[2]

- Contemporary brain research and its early applications over the past two decades, especially the work of Roger Sperry, Paul MacLean, Howard Gardner, Leslie Hart, Sally Springer and Georg Deutsch. See full Bibliography for exact references.

- Suggestopedia, a holistic model of learning and teaching developed by Bulgarian physician, psychiatrist and educational researcher, Georgi Lozanov.[3] In 1979 I received training in the art of Suggestopedia from Lozanov personally. This experience provided the stimulus for the development of my first language course applications using a methodology based on suggestion at the University of Massachusetts at Boston in the fall of 1979. Earlier forms of what I now am calling the ACT Approach are referred to in the literature on the subject as the "Lozanov Method," "Suggestopedia," the "S.A.L.T." (Suggestive-Accelerative Learning and Teaching) Approach, and the ACT Approach.

- The psycholinguistic research of Stephen Krashen[4] and James J. Asher[5] and the closely related applications of those theories in the Natural Approach, developed by Tracy Terrell[6] and the Total Physical Response Approach, developed by Asher.

The ACT Approach synthesizes the theories mentioned above in an attempt to create an optimal model for teaching and learning. More than that, however, it seeks to offer teachers a guide for developing themselves as masterful communicators and facilitators of learning. It is hoped that renewed joy and satisfaction for both teachers and students will be the result of this work.

ACKNOWLEDGEMENTS

The work of many of my colleagues has greatly enriched my perspective since I wrote the original manuscript. I would like to acknowledge Eric Jensen and Bobbi DePorter, co-founders of Supercamp, and again Eric as director of Turning Point for Teachers for leading the way with powerfully effective forms of innovation which I have had the opportunity to learn from and contribute to. I have been further influenced by the excellent work of Peter Kline, Lawrence Martel and John Grassi in the exciting field of integrative learning. Also, Howard Gardner's work on multiple intelligences has expanded the perspective of the ACT Approach.

I wish to acknowledge Dan Gee for his imaginative and delightful "mindmap" illustrations, which capture the spirit I was seeking. His address is 304 Cliff Street, Santa Cruz, California 95060.

CHAPTER 1

THE BRAIN AS BACKGROUND

Although the roots of the ACT Approach reach back into the depth psychology of Jung and the humanistic model of Psychosynthesis, it is our growing understanding of the human brain--how it functions, what affects it, how we can assist it--which has become the real foundation for the model described in this book. None of the humanistic concerns or the affective dimensions of learning are neglected by this focus upon brain function. Quite the contrary. As we find ways of creating environments that are brain-compatible--or rather--brain-enhancing, we serve the whole person in all his dimensions.

Right Brain / Left Brain

Following the Nobel Prize-winning work of Roger Sperry and others on the differing functions of the right and left hemispheres of the brain, a flood of literature has speculated as to the impact which different educational models or procedures may have on the two hemispheres. Traditional curricula and classroom approaches have been heavily criticized for appealing rather exclusively to the left hemisphere and neglecting the considerable resources of the right.[7]

It has been tempting for those who have popularized brain research to create neat, oversimplified dichotomies and to jab at educational straw men that they have erected. As respected a thinker as Robert

Ornstein, in *The Psychology of Consciousness*, asserted that we in the West have been using only half our brains, leaving half our potential untapped.[8] Such extreme formulations encourage further oversimplifications until we have the situation which Howard Gardner has colorfully described:

> It is becoming a familiar sight. Staring directly at the reader--frequently from a magazine cover--is an artist's rendition of the two halves of the brain. Surprinted athwart the left cerebral hemisphere (probably in stark blacks and grays) are such words as "logical," "analytical," and "Western rationality." More luridly etched across the right hemisphere (in rich orange or royal purple) are "intuitive," "artistic," or "Eastern consciousness." Regrettably, the picture says more about a current popular science vogue than it does about the brain.[9]

Indeed, the conclusion which the rapidly growing body of brain research leads us, is that since nearly all brain functions overlap, and since both hemispheres are so inter-connected and simultaneously involved in most complex human functioning, it is unwise to speak simplistically of left-brain or right-brain methods.

Lozanov states that

> in no case does the brain function only with its cortex structures, or only with the subcortex, or with only the right or the left hemisphere. The functional unity of the brain is unbreakable no matter that in some cases one activity or another comes to the fore.[10]

Lozanov's three "psychophysiological laws," upon which his work is based, reflect his integrated view of the brain:

1) the global participation of the brain
2) the simultaneous processes of analysis and synthesis
3) the simultaneous and indivisible participation of the
   conscious and para-conscious processes

Sally Springer and Georg Deutsch, in their serious, well-documented book, *Left Brain, Right Brain*, view with appropriate caution the facile popularization of theories about the two hemispheres. They show that existent research does not support a neat separation of mental functions to either of the hemispheres, since both hemispheres seem to be involved in nearly every behavior in the normal human being. They note that "our educational system may miss training or developing half of the brain, but it probably does so by missing out on the talents of both hemispheres."[11] Springer and Deutsch speak of "dichotomania" to characterize the glut of popular misinformation surrounding the brain.[12]

Exaggerations aside, however, there are, it seems to me, valuable nuggets of truth for the educator in the left brain / right brain debate, if only to alert us to important qualities we may have been neglecting. Springer and Deutsch list a group of dichotomies which are frequently attributed to left / right brain hemispheres:

Left Hemisphere	Right Hemisphere
Convergent	Divergent
Intellectual	Intuitive
Deductive	Imaginative
Rational	Metaphorical
Vertical	Horizontal
Discrete	Continuous
Abstract	Concrete
Realistic	Impulsive
Directed	Free
Differential	Existential
Sequential	Multiple
Historical	Timeless
Analytical	Holistic
Explicit	Tacit
Objective	Subjective
Successive	Simultaneous[13]

As educators we do not have to wait for researchers to demonstrate conclusively where the qualities are located in the brain. We agree that we want the qualities of both columns to infuse and inform the teaching and learning experience. It would be wiser, therefore, to talk less of hemispheric location and create more balanced, inclusively comprehensive educational experiences.

Carl Sagan, in his book, *The Dragons of Eden,* avoids trendy exaggerations about right/left hemispheres: "We might say that human culture is the function of the corpus callosum."[14] He thereby evokes the underlying unity of the brain in human endeavor and accomplishment.

Whatever their theoretical bias, most authors linking brain research to education urge a more global, comprehensive approach to learning. Rather than argue prematurely over which hemisphere is involved, it makes much more sense to focus on creating a richly varied instructional environment saturated with "authentic" input which engages as much of the brain as possible. Above all, it makes sense to do so in a climate which fosters imagination, adventure and risk-taking--where fear and anxiety are at a minimum. Such a position is strongly supported by the pioneering work of Leslie Hart.

The Theory of Leslie Hart

Leslie Hart's work I have found to be perhaps the most creative and helpful in translating the rapidly growing understanding of the brain into educational terms. In his book on brain function and brain-compatible education, *Human Brain, Human Learning*,[15] Hart offers a brilliant and practical theory for applying brain research to education. I would like to briefly sketch Hart's main ideas, because we will find them echoed or paralleled in Lozanov's, Asher's, Krashen's and Terrell's ideas about foreign language study. The implications of the following points will be readily apparent for foreign language programs whose major objective is authentic communication.

Hart, in *Human Brain and Human Learning*, argues that most formal educational environments are not very brain-compatible. In fact, they tend to be brain-antagonistic, pervaded as they are by over-structuring, over-control, over-confinement, lock-step, linear sequence--and above all by a fear of consequences if the established norms are not followed. Lozanov speaks equally strongly, referring to the "didactogeny" or school/teacher-caused maladies of both body and mind which pupils develop in antagonistic "educational" environments.[16] Without denigrating the good intentions which have unwittingly led to such a situation, it is important to see that as we learn more about the process of learning, old structures and strategies have often been based on wrong assumptions and ignorance. American education, so often the butt of scapegoating, can be appreciated for the great opportunities it has provided for so many. It can also be approached with resolve, in the spirit of flexible change which has been one of the most valuable virtues of American society in general.

Hart demonstrates that the human brain thrives on an input-rich environment rather than one "logically" organized by a well-meaning teacher. "It can be stated flatly," says Hart, "that the human brain is not organized or designed for linear, one-path thought," but rather "operates by simultaneously going down many paths."[17] He adds:

> Since the brain is indisputably a multipath, multimodal apparatus, the notion of mandatory sequences, or even of any fixed sequences, is unsupportable. Each of us learns in a personal, highly individual, mainly random way. . . . That being the case, any group instruction that has been tightly, logically planned will have been wrongly planned for most of the group, and will inevitably inhibit, prevent, or distort learning.[18]

Similarly, Lozanov advocates the natural, innate capacity of the brain to learn and laments the ignorance of many educators:

> Instead of creating conditions for the joyous satisfaction of personality's basic need--the thirst for information, and instead of bearing in mind the way the brain functions, teachers often seem to want to teach the brain how to function.[19]

In advocating following natural brain processes, Hart is not arguing against planning or structure but rather for the kind of massive input the brain thrives on:

> This learning process, being natural, appears effortless, but . . . it requires much random, fortuitous exposure and experience--input.[20]

What the brain does with the massive input, which "reality" provides, is to detect patterns and develop sophisticated programs for responding to them. The brain as "pattern detector" is for Hart the "first fundamental":

> There is no concept, no fact in education, more directly important than this: the brain is, by nature's design, an amazingly subtle and sensitive pattern-detecting apparatus.[21]

Learning to cooperate with the natural pattern-detecting capacity of the brain rather than imposing or forcing artificial patterns (such as occurs in most "educational" structuring) is a key challenge for educators today.

The brain detects, constructs, and elaborates patterns as a built-in and natural function. It does not have to be taught or motivated to do so any more than the heart needs to be instructed or coaxed to pump blood. In fact, efforts to teach or motivate the pattern detection, however well meant, may have inhibiting and negative effects.[22]

The implications of Hart's theories for educators are many, but perhaps the most obvious is the possibility of transforming our "low-input" classrooms into rich, multi-modal, reality-saturated environments, enabling the brain to do what comes naturally. Specifically, Hart recommends raising the quantity and quality of input for the learner by:

a. Increasing the number of hours during which input is provided....
b. Giving students exposure to and interaction with many people rather than very few, including a team of teachers, other staff, apprentices, volunteers, visitors, older students, peers and other helpers.

   c. Providing a great variety of machines, devices, equipment, and materials ... (and Hart goes on to list over 50 different kinds of aids for the learning environment).

   d. Offering hundreds of presentations to students in such forms as visitor's talks, exhibits, performances, films, filmstrips, demonstrations (actual rather than verbal). . . .

   e. Arranging many field trips. . .[23]

Hart maintains that "we do not have to worry about over-stimulation so long as the students select input rather than having it forced on them."[24]

High quality, high volume input is the raw material on which the brain thrives. It is one of the necessary conditions for optimal learning. A second condition is the opportunity to express oneself in relation to the input--specifically by talking.

> Students must talk and communicate to learn well. . . . a good command of language, an ability to convey ideas and information in speech and writing and to receive and understand communication is an essential body of skill to function well in almost any role in society.[25]

Unfortunately, as Hart points out, the irony is that "conventional schools expend a huge amount of energy and time suppressing talk."[26] Hart, as well as other present pioneers in FL communication,[27] mean by talk "an actual exchange" where "something happens." "Exercises are not communication."[28]

One of the essential functions of "talking" is to stimulate feedback, a third condition Hart sees necessary for optimal learning--feedback which will help learners "find out whether their pattern extraction and recognition is correct or improving, and whether programs have been appropriately selected and executed."[29] And the best feedback is, according to Hart, feedback from "reality" rather than from a teacher/authority, who tends to monitor performance from a "right" or "wrong" point of view. What the learner needs is to be guided and encouraged on the general track of acquisition as he acquires performance programs which require much trial and error.

> What is wanted . . . is feedback from reality rather than from an authority . . . Programs have to be acquired by progressively refining the initial crude and clumsy execution so that it becomes smoother and more exact after many trials. If the slow or halting or inaccurate early performance is called wrong, the feedback gives a false message. We build programs by having a correct general idea of what we are trying to do, and then gradually reducing error by getting and heeding feedback.[30]

"Reality feedback" stems from interaction in authentic life contexts, with real people, real machines, objects, etc. Most students draw a clear line between the classroom "world" and the "real" world outside. For years, foreign language educators from widely varying methodological persuasions have been calling for programs which produce "real" competence--a "real" ability to communicate in the target language, rather than the ability to pass tests "about" the language. More and more instruction approaches are attempting to increase "authentic" communication. Making communication authentic is a very challenging task, given the fixed mind-set which most students have toward classroom learning based on thousands of hours of experience. As we will later see, the ACT Approach seeks to offer some uniquely effective strategies to break through the mind-set of students, producing an authentic, full-spectrum experience by capitalizing on the power of the imagination.

Hart's fourth necessary condition for optimal, brain-compatible learning is the **absence of threat** in an environment where risk-taking is encouraged and safe. He sees the absence of threat as the prerequisite for the usefulness of the other three conditions. Hart presents evidence that complex creative human learning is possible due to the incredible evolution of the human cerebrum, the most recent part of the "triune" brain to develop. In order for the cerebrum to function maximally, it must not be under threat. When threat is experienced, "downshifting" occurs, and the "full use of the great new cerebral brain is suspended, and faster-acting, simpler brain resources take larger roles."[31] We are not talking here primarily of the more obvious overt, conscious verbal threats which teachers often make, but of the pervasive background of fear, against which many of our instructional programs operate--fear of failure, fear of appearing stupid, fear of authority, fear of consequences of all kinds.

Hart considers one of the most basic threats to students to be the physical confinement of the school and classroom environment--being forced to stay in a very small area under threat of fear-producing consequences. The implications for educational settings become clear:

> [since] virtually all academic and vocational learning heavily involves the neocortex, it becomes plain that absence of threat is utterly essential to effective instruction. Under threat, the cerebrum downshifts--in effect, to greater or lesser extent, it simply ceases to operate. To experienced teachers, this shutting down of the newest brain is an old story and a familiar frustration. The threatened child. . ."freezes," seems unable to think, stabs wildly at possible answers, breaks into tears, vomits, or acts up, perhaps to the point of violence.[32]

The examples, stories and effects of fear in the foreign language classroom are, of course, legion. As Hart adds, "since language exists almost wholly in the new brain, downshifting leaves us speechless, quite literally."[33] How silent many foreign language classrooms would be if the teacher would stop talking!

To sum up Hart's arguments:

- The human brain is a magnificent organ of learning developed over thousands of years for coping with the massive input which both external and internal stimuli provide. It does this by detecting patterns, remembering them, developing response programs and storing, retrieving, and revising these as circumstances require.

- The brain does not operate in a logical, linear fashion, but rather receives and processes stimuli multi-modally and simultaneously.

- The brain thrives on high-volume input. It learns naturally and easily under the appropriate conditions.

- Communication is a basic form of expression needed by the brain to actualize its potential and needed to generate feedback about the effectiveness of its programs. Speech, especially, is important--the ability to talk and understand.

- Feedback is essential for optimal brain functioning. For full brain learning, feedback which shows the individual that he is on the right track, moving toward meaningful goals--rather than categorical judgments of right or wrong--is necessary.

- Risk is an essential ingredient for optimal brain use. Risk, freely embraced, becomes a response to a built-in human urge to dare, to seek to go beyond the known. In contrast, threat, inflicted on the individual, creates fear and concomitant downshifting of the brain to more simplistic and inhibited response patterns.

As we shall see, the ACT Approach seeks to engage the whole person in learning large quantities of "real" material. It seeks to do this by creating a mentally relaxed, richly varied, non-stressful ambiance, skillfully guided and orchestrated by the teacher. When successfully applied, the approach assists students in accessing untapped learning potential with ease and enjoyment.

On the next page the reader will find a "mind map" – a pictorial summary of the main themes and concepts of this chapter. These non-linear, imagistic reviews conclude each chapter. They invite the reader to enter into non-linguistic experiences which, when wed with the previous reading, will produce a richer, more deeply encoded grasp and retention of the material.

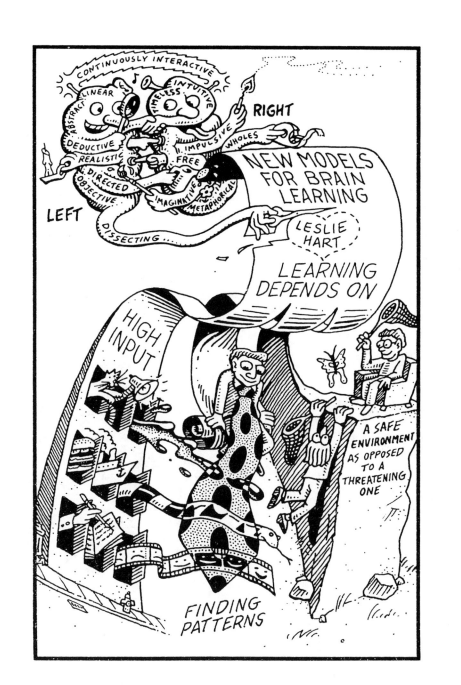

CHAPTER 2

THE CONTRIBUTION OF LOZANOV

No other single influence has been so decisive in the development of the ACT Approach as the work of Georgi Lozanov. A Bulgarian physician, psychiatrist and educational researcher, Lozanov has spent more than 30 years investigating and applying the phenomenon of suggestion in a wide range of learning contexts. His work has attracted attention in the West for the past two decades, and his influence continues to grow. The reader may refer to the relevant titles in the Bibliography for a comprehensive exposition of his theories and research.[34] The purpose of this chapter is to review the ideas which have made the most significant contribution to the ACT Approach.

The Mental Reserve Capacities

Lozanov repeatedly speaks of liberating man's extraordinary innate potential. His theory and methodological perspective focuses one-pointedly on that goal. In 1978 a UNESCO commission visited his research center in Sophia, Bulgaria, to observe and evaluate his work. His report to them begins:

> One of mankind's perennial aspirations has been to release man's reserve capacities and to stimulate their development.[35]

The Limiting Social Suggestive Norms

According to Lozanov, man's "reserve capacities" (or untapped potential) are not so much dormant as they are held in check by what Lozanov calls the socio-suggestive norms, i.e. our conditioning. These social and cultural norms project the sub-conscious attitudes and beliefs about ourselves and the world which limit our conception about what is real or possible. Suggestology, and its educational application, Suggestopedia, strive to provide the understanding and the means to liberate

> the pupil from fear and from the routine social suggestive norm of his limited powers . . . and create a system of sustained, continuous inner liberation. The pupil's confidence in his own capacities for learning should grow constantly and in this way instruction gradually develops into self-instruction. It will gradually go beyond the limitations of the social suggestive norm and penetrate into the sphere of human reserve capacities.[36]

The Key Principles of Suggestology

With the understanding of the human brain outlined in Chapter 1 as background, we can better appreciate Lozanov's "Suggestology"--those ideas which are the basis for Suggestopedia as an approach to learning and a cornerstone of the ACT Approach. Lozanov's three inseparable, fundamental principles of suggestology are in keeping in with Hart's theories of the brain as "pattern-detector."

- Interpersonal communication and mental activity are always conscious and paraconscious [read sub-conscious] at the same time.

- Every stimulus is associated, coded, symbolized and generalized.

- Every perception is complex.[37]

Without detailing the implications of these principles, one can see that Lozanov conceives of human interaction and learning in terms of mental processes. The brain, consciously and para-consciously receives, orders, codes, retrieves and utilizes the stimuli coming from the outside world in certain ways. Implied in these principles is Lozanov's holistic, global view of the personality which decisively affects his educational model. The first principle is clear as stated; under the second and third, Lozanov is pointing to the multi-leveled, complex nature of all the input from the external world. He underlines the notion that external stimuli are far too complex to manage or hold with only the mechanisms of our conscious attention. His somewhat technical assumptions form the basis for his ideas about how to tap the sub-conscious--or as he calls it, the para-conscious--levels of our experience. Once we know how to do that, he argues, then we have acquired the tools for tapping our extraordinary mental reserves.

The Role of Suggestion

The greatest contribution of Lozanov is his deep insight into what functions as suggestive to the mind: the conditioning or de-conditioning effect of the multi-leveled input which we are constantly receiving.

> Suggestion is a constant communicative factor which chiefly through paraconscious mental activity can create conditions for tapping the functional reserve capacities of personality.[38]

Thus, of key importance, as we will see in detail later, is his view that suggestion

- operates as a **constant** communicative factor in all interchange;

- operates largely at the sub-conscious level;

- can become a powerful means for helping students achieve more of their potential.

As we teachers become aware of how we are affecting our students' experience and performance, we can choose to become increasingly helpful and effective embodiers of suggestion. The task is first one of becoming aware of ourselves as potent carriers of multitudinous suggestions, and second, one of transforming and aligning our suggestive impact in order to be congruent with the purposes we wish to serve.

The Anti-Suggestive Barriers

Before outlining how suggestion can help us unlock untapped potential, mention needs to be made of the chief barrier against any purposeful use of the suggestive process. According to Lozanov, the ingrained, limiting attitudes and beliefs which each of us to some degree possesses, result largely from our childhood conditioning.

> There is no suggestion without desuggestion, without freeing paraconsciousness from the inertia of something old.[39]

The kinds of "barriers" to which Lozanov is referring all have one commonality, that is, they operate to protect the seemingly safe and trustworthy status quo. To overcome them successfully is not to confront these barriers with something fearfully foreign, but, as Lozanov writes, "through harmonization with them."[40] Neuro-Linguistic Programming, a communication model which runs strikingly parallel to Lozanov's work, refers to this harmonization process as the condition of "establishing rapport."[41] This and related processes, including the means of suggestion referred to in the next paragraph, will be discussed at length in the later sections on the ACT Approach.

Lozanov's Means of Suggestion

The Suggestive means which can be used to stimulate openness to learning appear to be nearly unlimited. Lozanov emphasizes several key suggestive factors available in the teaching situation:

- **Authority:** the prestige, the trustworthiness, the presence of personality projected by the teacher as well as the prestige, credibility, impression of the learning institution itself--are powerful suggestive carriers. All that is associated with such factors will have authoritative, impressioning impact. How to cultivate appropriate authority and trustworthy presence rather than authoritarianism is of major concern in the ACT Approach.

- Evoking **a child-like, playful state** in the students (Lozanov uses the infelicitous term "infantilization") is an effective means of tapping into reserve capacities. Its potency is closely connected to the degree of positive authority which the teacher is able to embody.

- **Pseudopassivity** is a highly receptive, mentally relaxed state which students are easily able to experience and process information in the musical, concert-like presentations of material.

- **Doubleplaneness** is a term Lozanov coined to describe the multiple levels which are operating during any communicational exchange. He is above all concerned with the factors which are operating below the threshold of consciousness but which are nevertheless exerting an often decisive suggestive impact. Such factors are numerous and include facial expression, voice intonation, pitch and rhythm, posture, etc.

- **Peripheral stimuli** can function decisively in any carefully orchestrated suggestopedic environment:

By "peripheral perceptions" Lozanov is referring to stimuli which

> at the moment of perceiving have got into the periphery of attention and
> consciousness. They do not fall in the focus of consciousness because of
> its limited volume. . . Having reached the brain, this information emerges
> in the consciousness with some delay . . . and is operative in tapping the
> reserve capacities. This peripheral information included in the
> paraconsciousness underlies long term memory.[42]

Such things as graphic illustrations, posters and charts which contain an interwoven mixture of informational and pictorial stimuli are cited
as effective carriers of peripherally perceived material which is subconsciously registered and later recalled when activated in the context of the
larger whole.

Lozanov reports several experiments where he gave students a list
of names to learn--requiring conscious focus of attention. He included peripheral information such as an instructional heading or color underlining
which students were not asked to learn or note. Subsequent testing showed
that the material consciously focused on was forgotten at a rate predictable according to the so-called Ebbinghaus curve of forgetting. By contrast, the peripherally perceived information was recalled in a statisti-
cally significant rise in recollection.

> Having once entered the brain, there is a delay before [the peripheral
> information] floats up in the consciousness . . . Our studies have shown
> that this peripheral unconscious information rests at the basis of long-
> term memory.[43]

Lozanov's Suggestopedia

Suggestopedy or suggestopedia is what Lozanov terms the pedagogical application of Suggestology. When correctly implemented, asserts
Lozanov, suggestopedia embodies the following characteristics:

- Memory reserves, intellectual activity reserves, creativity reserves and the
  reserves of the whole personality are tapped. If we do not release many-
  sided reserve capacities we cannot speak of suggestopedia.

- Instruction is always accompanied with an effect of relaxation or, at least,
  one without a feeling of fatigue. If pupils get tired in lessons, we cannot
  speak of suggestopedia.

- Suggestopedic teaching and learning is always a pleasant experience.

- It always has a favorable educational effect, softening aggressive tendencies in pupils and helping them to adapt themselves to society.

- A significant . . . psychotherapeutic effect can be observed .[44]

Lozanov lists three main principles of suggestopedia:

- Joy, absence of tension and concentrative psychorelaxation.

- Unity of the conscious-paraconscious and integral brain activation.

- Suggestive relationship on the level of the reserve complex.[45]

By "joy" Lozanov means the delight and pleasure which accompanies authentic learning, the experience of new understanding, new breadth, new power, new competence and new self-esteem all within an experiential context of "calmness, steadiness, inner confidence and trust."[46] Note, in no way is "joy" defined as simply giving a pleasant veneer to the learning experience:

> joy springs not so much from the pleasant outward organization of the educational process, but rather from the easy assimilation of the material and the easy way it can be used in practice.[47]

His second principle refers to the holistic, global nature of the learning experience. Both the conscious and unconscious, the analytic and synthetic dimensions of the educational process are engaged as simultaneously as possible.

His principle of "suggestive relationship" is subtle and crucial, for it is, in a sense, his unifying principle. Lozanov is referring to the need to maintain the focus on his over-arching objective of tapping reserve capacities. This means learning to apply the various principles in fine attunement with the underlying purposes of the method; and, to use as steady feedback, the degree to which the reserves are being reached. That is, if the characteristics of joy, ease and rapid learning are not observed, the reserves, by definition, are not being reached.

The Means of Lozanov's Suggestopedia

Lozanov describes three major types of suggestopedic means: 1) psychological, 2) didactic, and 3) artistic. The psychological means focus on the teacher's skill in maintaining the appropriate suggestive atmosphere while focusing on the goal of tapping the reserve capacities of the students.

> The teacher should be a master of the art of connecting the peripheral perceptions and the emotional stimulus in all-round orchestration with the globally presented material. . . In the process of teaching students

how to learn, the teacher must not only give them the respective material, but he must also teach them how to help themselves in learning it.[48]

The didactic means refer to the structural design and integration of
the course elements. Thus the teacher strives for global, meaningful inter-
connections and offers a large amount of relevant material. Much of the
material and much specific information is orchestrated to be received
through the "second plane" (paraconscious level) rather than drilled for
step by step conscious mastery. In teaching foreign languages, for instance,

> the students' attention is directed to the whole sentence, to its meaning-
> ful communicative aspect, to its place and role in the given amusing life
> situation. At the same time pronunciation, vocabulary and grammar
> remain to a great extent on a second plane. They are also assimilated
> but the well-trained teacher draws the students' attention to them only
> for a short time and then goes back quickly to the sense of the whole
> sentence and situation. A considerable part of these elements are
> learned along with the whole structure without any special attention be-
> ing paid to them.[49]

The "artistic" means have probably received the most attention
from outside observers of suggestopedia, since they are easily perceived as
unique:

> The artistic means of suggestopedia introduce a special kind of liberat-
> ing and stimulating didactic art (music, literature, acting, etc.) into the
> process of teaching and learning. They are not an illustrative stage in
> the process of learning, **but are built in to the contents of the les-
> son** (my emphasis). They promote the suggestopedic psychological
> orchestration by introducing, on the second plane, an abundance of
> harmonized peripheral perceptions.[50]

Among the most striking artistic means used in suggestopedia are
music and role-play. The ACT Approach incorporates both, and the specific procedures are described and discussed at length in later sections.

In sum:

Lozanov presents both a global theory of learning and set of strategies for helping students realize their potential. He provides a framework
for allowing the teacher to begin to tap the powerful sub-conscious resources we all possess both as teachers and learners. The results he reports
in Bulgarian applications for both adult foreign language programs and
children's reading and primary level math curricula are quite dramatic.
These applications have sparked the desire of many educators throughout
the world to attempt to duplicate or adapt his programs. Unfortunately,
due to a repressive political situation in Bulgaria, Lozanov remained

inaccessible to the West from 1979 to 1989. As a result, like-minded pioneers or interpreters were forced to proceed on their own. Although Lozanov's inaccessibility was regrettable, it did provide a positive stimulus for others, myself included, to develop further creative variations. Lozanov is now, as of this writing, able to travel freely and is once again in active contact with Western educators.

The ACT Approach is heavily indebted to Lozanov, although it recognizes that his model needs to be wed with American pedagogical reality. ACT also recognizes and incorporates many invaluable contributions made by American educators, seeking a synthesis in order to provide teachers and students with a holistic model for teaching and learning which is both effective and enjoyable.

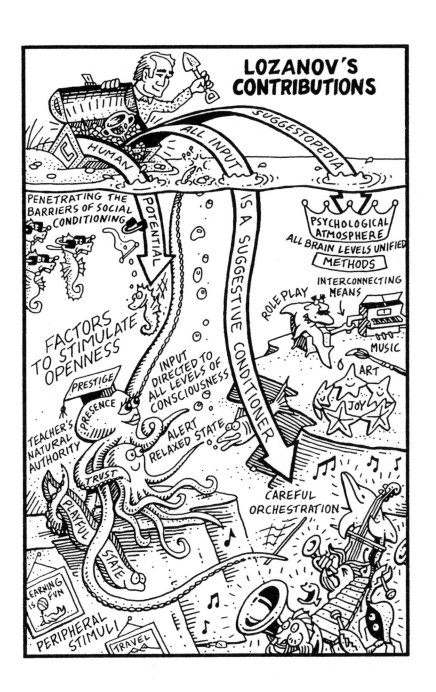

CHAPTER 3

LANGUAGE ACQUISITION / LANGUAGE LEARNING
The Pioneering Work of Krashen, Asher and Terrell

The Work of Stephen Krashen

It might seem surprising that a field as traditional as that of foreign languages has become an active testing ground for applying the frontier work of both Lozanov and contemporary brain researchers. Lozanov, whose interest is not primarily in foreign language pedagogy, but in the learning and teaching process itself chose foreign languages as a demonstration model for his theories on suggestion. In his decision to develop a suggestopedic instructional model to teach adults a new foreign language in a short period of time, he gained an opportunity to demonstrate several ideas:

- that a large quantity of information might be effectively learned in a short period of time (a 1500-2000 word vocabulary in 5 weeks / 75 hours);
- that the limiting socio-cultural bias that adults cannot learn foreign languages can be overcome;
- that both preceding objectives can be accomplished with ease, no homework, and no fatigue;
- that there could be significant psychological and physiological health benefits accompanying students' success in tapping more of their potential.[51]

The dramatic results he has reported in his adult foreign language courses has become inspiration to many as well as the stuff of sensational journalism for others.[52] Yet Lozanov's influence on American foreign language education has been slow in coming. Few people are directly acquainted with his work, a fact due at least in part to the professional jargon of East European social sciences, resulting in language which tends to render his writings somewhat obscure. His geographical/political isolation, the resulting absence of his leadership, and scanty or inconclusive data demonstrating the methodological effectiveness of Suggestopedia in America, have further contributed to a wait and see attitude among language teachers. The Society for Accelerative Learning and Teaching has made an invaluable contribution toward "Americanizing" Lozanov,[53] yet the potential significance of Lozanov's work for foreign language pedagogy still waits to be realized.

A valuable bridge between the originality of Lozanov and the American foreign language teaching profession is the provocative work of Stephen Krashen. Krashen, a psycholinguist at the University of Southern California, has offered a set of hypotheses on the acquisition of second languages. His work has made a decisive contribution to the development of the A C T Approach and also helps to explain in part why Lozanov's FL model can be so effective.

Krashen's Five Hypotheses:

I. The Acquisition-Learning Hypothesis

This hypothesis draws a distinction between language acquisition and language learning; these are the two means available to adults for developing competence in a second language. According to Krashen, acquisition is essentially a subconscious process through which we comprehend and respond within the vast complexity of language form and possibilities.

> Language acquirers are usually not aware of the fact that they are acquiring language, but are only aware of the fact that they are using the language for communication.[54]

The fluency of speaking any language is, for example, a process so complex that it exceeds our capacity for conscious control. It is governed by patterns we have acquired and also use subconsciously. Thus, according to Krashen's distinction, speaking is not consciously "learned" like one learns the alphabet--it is "acquired."

Language **learning**, in contrast to acquisition, is a conscious phenomenon. "Language learning is 'knowing about' language," referring to "'explicit' knowledge of rules, being aware of them and being able to talk about them."[55]

Viewed from the perspective of the acquisition/learning hypothesis, it is clear that language teaching in the vast majority of classes is directed toward language learning. Krashen cites considerable research to support his assertion that the conscious study of grammar rules and language structure does not help the process of language acquisition. If these assertions are valid, the implications for language teaching are profound. As the language teaching profession continues to move toward the objective of "communicative competence" as top priority, the question of whether to stress conscious learning about language or to create an environment where the "natural" process of acquisition can take place becomes crucial. The ACT Approach gives first priority to language acquisition and, although language "learning" is not neglected, its role at the beginning level is modest.

Krashen's hypothesis about the subconscious nature of language acquisition helps explain why Lozanov has been able to achieve remarkable teaching results. The overriding goal of Suggestopedia has been to liberate the subconscious resources available to students through the skillful use of suggestion. The narrower objective of Lozanov's language program has been to help students develop the capacity to communicate sucessfully in authentic situations--rather than to pass grammar tests on the language.[56]

Krashen presents the following comparison between learning and acquisition:

The Acquisition-Learning Distinction

Acquisition	Learning
• Similar to child's first language acquisition	• Formal knowledge of language
• "Picking up" a language	• "Knowing about" a language
• Subconscious	• Conscious
• Implicit knowledge	• Explicit knowledge
• Formal teaching does not help	• Formal teaching helps[57]

II. The Natural Order Hypothesis

Krashen's second hypothesis is that "grammatical structures are acquired (not necessarily learned) in a predictable order."[58] He cites numerous studies which provide evidence to support the assertion that both children and adults, in first and second language acquisition, respectively, acquire grammatical structures according to an inherent, "natural" order, and that conscious intervention or the willful superimposing of another order will be minimally effective before the student is "ready." Krashen does not, however, advocate teaching grammar according to a "natural order." Not enough is yet known about such an order to allow any kind of comprehensive plan. More importantly, according to Krashen, no conscious sequencing of grammar is necessary for successful language acquisition to occur.[59]

This hypothesis underscores both the natural and subconscious nature of language acquisition. Its implications for teaching are significant. We may well be able to spare our students the considerable effort necessary to learn specific grammatical structures at a particular point in their study, (most frequently the result of following the grammar presentation of the text in use). Indeed, the conscious study of grammar may well have little or no value to our students, if the course goal is language acquisition. This brings us to Krashen's third hypothesis.

III. The Monitor Hypothesis

This hypothesis states:

"Conscious learning has an extremely limited function in adult second language performance: it can only be used as a Monitor, or an editor."[60]

According to Krashen, communicative fluency functions subconsciously, and speech is initiated not by our conscious censor, but "by the acquired system . . . We can use the Monitor to make changes in our utterances only after the utterance has been generated by the acquired system."[61]

What a student may have "learned" in class will, at the conscious level, be of limited use. Indeed, three requirements must be satisfied, asserts Krashen, if the Monitor is to be used successfully in fluent communication:

- *The performer has to have enough time.* In rapid conversation, taking time to think about rules, such as the subjunctive or subject-verb agreement, may disrupt communication.

- *The performer has to be thinking about correctness or be focused on form.* Even when we have time, we may not be concerned with whether we have inflected the verb correctly! We may be more concerned with what we are saying and not how we are saying it.

- *The performer has to know the rule.*[62]

Most foreign language programs focus nearly exclusively on creating highly trained "monitor users." The danger is to encourage overuse of the monitor.

> *Monitor Over-users* . . . are people who attempt to monitor all the time, performers who are constantly checking their output with their conscious knowledge of the second language. As a result, such performers may speak hesitantly, often self-correct in the middle of utterances, and are so concerned with correctness that they cannot speak with any real fluency.[63]

The "monitor over-user" is all too familiar to most FL teachers. "Conversation" courses abound with them--much to everyone's frustration. The lesson of Krashen, of Lozanov, and, as we shall see, of Asher and of Terrell, is to keep the focus off analysis and conscious control and instead, to tap the students' subconscious capacities. We do not wish to ignore our conscious capacities; we want to produce neither monitor over-users or under-users.

The goal of the ACT Approach is "the optimal Monitor users," who, in Krashen's definition:

> use the Monitor when it is appropriate and when it does not interfere with communication. Many optimal users will not use grammar in ordinary conversation, where it might interfere. (Some very skilled performers, such as some professional linguists and language teachers, might be able to get away with using considerable amounts of conscious knowledge in conversation . . . but this is very unusual.) In writing, and in planned speech, however, when there is time, optimal users will typically make whatever corrections they can to raise the accuracy of their output.[64]

Thus, we wish to encourage the use of the Monitor as an appropriate supplement--not as an interference--to one's acquired competence.

IV. The Input Hypothesis

With this hypothesis Krashen states that:

> we acquire (not learn) language by understanding input that is a little beyond our current level of (acquired) competence . . . The input hypothesis claims that listening comprehension and reading are of primary importance in the language program, and that the ability to speak (or write) fluently in a second language will come on its own with time. Speaking fluency is thus not "taught" directly; rather, speaking ability "emerges" after the acquirer has built up competence through comprehending input.[65]

By input, Krashen is speaking of authentic target language which is comprehensible. Acquisition will automatically take place if the condition is met that the comprehensible language input contain the next stage or level in the "natural order" of the acquisition process. Krashen calls this input which contains "i + 1" (input which contains "the next step along the natural order"). The language input needs to be rich enough in contextual clues so that the student can easily and naturally make the growth stretch to the next level of competence.

An important corollary to this hypothesis is that input need not be finely tuned to the specific level of the student:

> In practice, providing optimal input may be surprisingly easy. It may be that all the teacher need do is make sure the students understand what is being said or what they are reading. When this happens, when the input is understood, if there is enough input, i + 1 will usually be covered automatically. Other structures will, of course, be present in the input as well, but there will be plenty of exposure to the i + 1 as well as a review of previously acquired structures.[66]

Primary sources of useful input for second language acquisition are **foreigner talk** (the modified speech native speakers will use when talking to non-natives), **teacher talk**, (foreigner talk designed for the classroom), **interlanguage talk**, (the speech of other second language acquirers). According to Krashen, "teacher talk" may or may not facilitate second language acquisition depending on its focus. In grammar-based approaches the teacher may tend to focus input narrowly, "finely tuned" to the specific grammar points and to exercises being introduced with the text.

The implications of recognizing the advantages of "roughly tuned input" are startling for many teachers, for they run counter to much of our professional conditioning. For years we have been drilling grammar, testing grammar, struggling for precise production, and experiencing frustration with student frustration. All the while we may well have been neglecting the most valuable resource of all: **ourselves**, as broad, engaging, authentic and comprehensible language sources. I know that for many years I withheld much of the range and richness of my language and informational competence in the interest of "getting through the text and the exercises." Krashen's hypotheses suggest that if we consider language acquisition to be our primary objective, such a conscious, task-oriented focus may be counter-productive. How many of us have felt guilty, in spite of the spark of interest lighting up our students' faces, when we have lapsed into personal stories, cultural anecdotes, or current issues, to the neglect of the exercises which would be reflected on the grammar test!

Krashen's input hypothesis pointedly validates teachers "talking" rather than drilling:

> When we "just talk" to our students, **if they understand,** we are not only giving a language lesson, we may be giving the best possible language lesson since we will be supplying input for acquisition.[67]

"Roughly tuned input," i.e. language designed to facilitate authentic communication, has, according to Krashen, several distinct advantages over the finely tuned input of many grammar-based orientations:

> With rough tuning, we are always assured that i + 1 will be covered, while with finely tuned exercises, we are taking a guess as to where the student is. With roughly tuned input, we are assured of constant recycling and review; this is not the case with "lock-step" exercises. Third, roughly tuned input will be good for more than one acquirer at a time, even when they are at slightly different levels. Finally, roughly tuned teacher talk or foreigner talk will nearly always be more interesting than an exercise that focuses on one grammatical point.[68]

V. The Affective Filter Hypothesis

By "affective filter" Krashen is referring to the affective factors which may block or facilitate acquisition. He cites numerous studies to support his assertions that learning environments which encourage self-confidence, high motivation and low anxiety facilitate language acquisition. "A low filter means that the performer is more 'open' to the input, and the input strikes 'deeper'. . ."[69] By keeping the "affective filter," which can impede language acquisition, low, two positive effects result:

- [positive attitudinal variables] actually encourage input; people who are motivated and who have a positive selfimage will seek and obtain more input;

• they contribute to a lower filter; given two acquirers with the exact same input, the one with a lower filter will acquire more.[70]

The second point has great significance for the conception and creation of our classroom environment, a question which will receive extensive exploration later in the discussion of the ACT Approach. Krashen states clearly that "our pedagogical goals should not only include supplying optimal input, but also creating a situation that promotes a low filter."[71]

In discussing how decisive the affective dimension can be for successful language acquisition, Krashen is echoing Lozanov's call for a learning environment characterized by positive support and a non-stressful atmosphere and also Hart's urging that educational settings be made free of "threat," yet encourage risk-taking.

In a point related to his above hypotheses, Krashen raises a question of great importance to most FL teachers, especially those who teach adults: is language learning a matter of aptitude? Language teachers frequently ask themselves and are asked by others: "Don't some just have the innate ability whereas others don't?" Krashen cites research evidence to challenge the evidence often used to support the assertion that students who do better on language aptitude tests do, in fact, perform better in FL classes. He believes that for classes which focus on language "learning," such aptitude tests may be an indicator of probable performance, and he concludes that aptitude is a factor which relates to "learning."[72]

For language acquisition, however, **attitude**, rather than aptitude, seems to be a more crucial factor. This may explain why students with a measured low "aptitude" for language learning may perform very well in a language acquisition environment, where their attitude may be highly positive. This hypothesis has significant implications for language teachers. What it means is that language acquisition may not be determined by "innate" factors such as aptitude, which cannot be influenced. Skillful teachers can decidedly affect student attitude, and the appropriate attitude is now seen as a crucial factor in successful language acquisition. As we shall later see, the ACT Approach centrally concerns itself with the creation of an instructional environment which fosters optimal student attitude.

Krashen supports his five hypotheses with broad evidence drawn from contemporary linguistic research. More important to most of us than a final judgment as to their validity is the question: does the model they suggest actually work? In my own experience this model provides a theoretical framework in linguistic terms to help explain the effectiveness of both Lozanov's holistic model and the ACT Approach. I was unaware of Krashen's work when I first began using the first variants of the ACT Approach at the University of Massachusetts. For the Fort Devens project, discussed in Chapter 13, I was able to integrate Krashen's hypotheses consciously into the course design. The results of this program provide a further example supportive of his theoretical proposals.

Of even broader significance, Krashen's work succeeds in helping language pedagogy catch up to the frontier of learning research. In Krashen's input hypothesis we can recognize a parallel to Hart's call for massive, rich and varied input, (not logically sequenced) for optimal brain functioning. We can also see similarities to Lozanov's foreign language model, which globally presents large quantities of material with attention paid to context (multi-modal, suggestive), and with little regard for grammatical sequencing. I would venture to characterize all three positions as a deep, emerging trend: an acknowledgement of the extraordinary capacities beyond consciousness, along with a search and reach for ways to tap those resources. Whether these authors speak in terms of brain capacity, paraconscious resources or subconscious language acquisition processes, we can find a common recognition of both the potential and determining force of subconscious resources.

Thus, in education, traditionally a field focusing nearly exclusively on cultivating consciousness, we find pioneers who are pointing to the subconscious as the next educational frontier waiting to be explored. The great forerunners in depth psychology, such as Freud, Jung and Assagioli, have led the way in turning our heads to processes which elude conscious control. Hart, Lozanov, Krashen and others of similar vision, are among the leaders continuing to explore beyond the limits of consciousness for answers about how we learn and how we can best facilitate learning. The ACT Approach embraces this new perspective on learning and seeks a methodology which will synthesize our conscious and subconscious abilities--for both teachers and students.

Two Sucessful Models for Second Language Acquisition

The Total Physical Response Approach (TPR)

James J. Asher, the developer of the Total Physical Response Approach (TPR), postulates that the second language acquisition process parallels first language acquisition. Asher maintains that the acquisition of a person's first language is greatly facilitated by the commands and physical responses which accompany the early exposure to language.[73]

The approach simulates, at a speeded up pace, the stages an infant experiences in acquiring its first language. For example, before the infant utters anything more intelligible than "Mommy" or "Daddy," that child has experienced hundreds of hours in which language was imprinted upon body movements. The infant may only be able to decode the language through the medium of body movements such as looking, laughing, pointing, reaching, touching, and eating. Understanding of the target language was achieved in thousands of intimate caretaking transactions in which adults gently directed the infant's behavior with sentences such as:

> Look at Daddy.
> Look at Grandpa.
> Smile for Grandpa.
> Point to Auntie.
> Touch your nose.
> Stick out your tongue.

Notice that these transactions do not demand speech from children. The child responds exclusively with a physical action initially and later in development with simple one-word utterances such as "yes" or "no."[74]

Thus, the hallmark of TPR is the physical enactment of commands given by the teacher and/or other students. Asher describes his basic classroom procedure as follows:

> The instructional strategy, which I call TPR, is to seat a few students on either side of the instructor and request, "When I say something in the target language, listen carefully and do what I do. For Example, if I say 'Tate!' and I stand up, you stand up. Just listen and act rapidly without trying to pronounce the words yourself."
>
> Then with the instructor as a model, the students start responding with actions to one-word commands such as "stand, sit, walk, stop, turn, and run." Most everyone is surprised that they can demonstrate perfect understanding with body movements in a few trials. Then the one-word sentence is expanded into:
>
> "Stand up; point to the door; walk to the door; touch it; and open the door!"
>
> Students are impressed that within a few minutes their comprehension can be expanded rapidly. Within a few hours, students understand grammatical constructions that are nested in the imperative such as:
>
> "When Maria walks to Juan and hits him on the arm, Shirou will run to the chalkboard and draw a funny picture of the instructor."[75]

Asher, like Krashen and Terrell, holds to the basic tenet that comprehension precedes production, and all recommend an essentially "silent" period of 10-15 hours during which a reservoir of comprehended input builds rapidly, providing the basis for the later <u>natural</u> emergence of speaking.

Asher characterizes TPR's guiding principles as follows:

- Understanding the spoken language should be developed in advance of speaking.

- Understanding should be developed through movements of the student's body. The imperative is a powerful aid because the instructor can utter commands to manipulate students behavior. Our research suggests that most of the grammatical structure of the target language and hundreds of vocabulary items can be learned through the skillful use of the imperative by the instructor.

- Do not attempt to force speaking from students. As the students internalize a cognitive map of the target language through understanding what is heard, there will be a point of readiness to speak. The individual will spontaneously begin to produce utterances.[76]

In my own experience TPR has shown itself to be a highly successful strategy, especially for the earliest stages of second language acquisition. I have integrated much of the TPR framework into the A C T Approach. Student motivation and confidence are quickly heightened as students succeed in demonstrating their comprehension through physical movements. Asher has also given us an excellent tool for engaging our students' physical energies, so lamentably neglected in most educational settings. The physical aspect alone helps raise student interest and motivational levels. The playful nature of the commands and responses makes this technique very compatible with the ACT Approach, which, as we shall see, actively exploits play and fantasy.

Finally, TPR is a relatively easy strategy to master and integrate into a wide variety of teaching approaches. Asher's own book and several others by his adherents offer detailed guidance for practical application.[77]

As with any approach, the "how" is usually more important than the "what". How sensitively an instructor uses TPR is crucial. Many if not most individuals are sensitive to power and authority and do not like being told what to do. The focus on the imperative form in TPR requires a skillful teacher to create a cooperative, playful atmosphere, where students feel at ease and willing to join in fully. An authoritarian intonation can easily sabotage the potential effectiveness of TPR. This crucial aspect of "how" to evoke a playful, effective atmosphere lies at the heart of the ACT Approach and will be discussed at length in the next chapters.

The Natural Approach

Originally developed by Tracy Terrell, the Natural Approach is designed to develop basic communicative skills. The approach has taken on added theoretical depth through close collaboration with Stephen Krashen. The jointly authored book, **The Natural Approach,** by Krashen and Terrell is an excellent resource for anyone interested in learning about and facilitating second language acquisition. The theoretical foundation of the Natural Approach is essentially covered by the five hypotheses of Krashen presented earlier in this chapter, although in practice, Terrell takes a more moderate position than does Krashen with his radical hypotheses. Terrell sees a more important role for language "learning" than does Krashen. Whereas Krashen seems to focus more exclusively on the unconscious acquisition process, Terrell attempts to provide a greater balance between conscious and unconscious strategies.

Terrell states the following basic principles for the Natural Approach:

- Focus of instruction is on communication rather than its form.
- Speech production comes slowly and is <u>never</u> forced.
- Early speech goes through natural stages (yes or no response, one-word answers, list of words, short phrases, complete sentences.)[78]

Terrell characterizes the Natural Approach as follows:

- Teacher creates situations in which students are motivated to communicate.
- Input must be interesting.
- What is said is comprehensible.
- Understanding is more important than speaking.
- Vocabulary development is more important than structural accuracy.
- Absence of error correction
- Low anxiety[79]

Terrell understands acquisition activities to be those which focus on message or meaning, and he classifies them into four types (some of these activities will be appropriate for early and/or later stages, which will be discussed later):

- Content (culture, subject matter, new information, reading, e.g. teacher tells interesting anecdote involving cultural contrast between target and native culture.)

- Affective-humanistic (students' own ideas, opinions, experiences, e.g. students are asked to share their personal preferences as to music, place to live, clothes, hair styles, etc.)

- Games [focus on using language to participate in the game, e.g. 20 questions: I, the teacher, am thinking of an object in this room. You, students, have 20 questions to guess object. Typical questions: is it clothing? (yes) is it for a man or a woman? (woman) is it a skirt? (yes) is it brown? (yes) is it Ellen's skirt? (yes)]

- Problem solving (focus on using language to locate information, use information, etc., e.g. looking at this listing of films in the newspaper, and considering the different tastes and schedule needs in the group, which film would be appropriate for all of us to attend, and when?)[80]

Terrell sees the language acquisition process as proceeding in a sequence of natural stages, the first of which is **comprehension**. To insure the development of retained comprehension, Terrell suggests creating "activities designed to teach students to recognize the meaning of words used in communicative contexts (=**binding**)." By "binding" Terrell means a sufficiently strong association between a new word and a referent, that the meaning is clear and held. Some "binding" techniques are more effective than others. For example, Terrell recommends Asher's TPR to aid in the binding process. The sounds a student hears when the instructor says: "Setzen Sie sich auf den Boden!" (Sit on the floor!) is likely to be more firmly "bound" and remembered when the the students actually sits on the floor in response to the command, than if the instructor were simply to tell the student that the words mean: "sit on the floor."

As a further way of binding, Terrell recommends teaching students to "guess at the meaning of utterances without knowing all of the words used and without knowing all of the grammatical structures of the sentences." To facilitate this associational binding process, Terrell advocates the use of extensive contextual aids for comprehension. Specifically, he advises using visual aids (pictures, realia, gestures), modifying (slowing, emphasizing) speech, and, particularly for adults, writing key vocabulary on chalkboard.

Stage 1, the Comprehension Stage. Typical activities:

- Total Physical Response (TPR).

- Supplying comprehensible input based on items in the class-room or brought to class. (Who has the ball? Who is wearing a green blouse?)

- Supplying comprehensible input based on pictures. Terrell counsels teachers to develop a "picture file," e.g. folders with large colorful pictures cut from magazines, categorized as "men," "women," "family relationships," "sports," "food," etc. Then, the teacher can, for instance, hold up pictures of a beautiful young woman and an old man and begin talking about them in a variety of comprehensible ways, e.g.: This is a man – an old man. This is a woman– a young woman. The man is wearing a hat. The woman is wearing a dress. Who is wearing the hat, the man or the woman? Who is young? Who is old. Who in the class is young? Who in the class is old (teacher can point to him/herself).

Typical ways students are encouraged to respond in the Comprehension Stage:

- An action (TPR): Stand up, go to the board, and draw a circle with a dot in the middle. The name of a fellow student: Who in the class is wearing a purple shirt? (John)

- Gestures: How is John feeling now, since his car broke down? Students hang heads down, make faces of depression, anger, frustration, etc.

- Students say yes/no in the target language: Is this woman in the picture old and ugly? Is this man an American million-aire?

- Students point to item or picture: Where is the person wearing a green skirt? Who is the most intelligent person in this picture? Where is the marker with the red top?

Stage 2, Early Speech

This stage commences "when students begin *accessing* and producing words and grammatical forms which have previously been *bound* through communicative interaction with contextualized input." Terrell asserts that in a Natural Approach environment, most adults will move voluntarily into Stage 2 within 2-10 hours of instruction.

Typical ways of early speech production:

- yes/no answers
- one-word answers
- lists of words
- two word strings and short phrases

In order to facilitate the transition from Stage 1 to Stage 2, instructors may use some of the following question techniques:

- Yes/no questions (Is Jimmy wearing a sweater today?)

- Choice questions (Is this a pencil or an eraser? Eraser.)

- Questions which can be answered with a single word. (What does the woman have in her hand? Book. Also Where? When? Who?--questions.)

- General questions which encourage lists of words (What do we see on the table now?)

- Open sentences with pause for student response (Mike is wearing a blue shirt, but Ron is wearing a _____ shirt.)

Stage 3, Speech Emergence

Terrell asserts that "after sufficient comprehensible input and opportunities to produce the target language in an affectively positive environment, speech production will normally improve in both quantity and quality." This stage is characterized by a developmental progression moving through the following forms of production:

- three words and short phrases
- longer phrases
- complete sentences where appropriate
- dialog
- extended discourse (discussion)
- narration

Activities at this stage will be both oral and written, and the student can begin more cognitively demanding tasks involving reading and

writing and the study of literature and culture. Among the activities
which Terrell suggest for this stage are:

- preference ranking (What are your favorite leisure
  time activities? What kinds of movies do you like
  best?)
- games of all sorts
- problem solving using charts, tables, graphs, maps
  (Looking at this train schedule, how can we be in
  Washington, D.C. for dinner and stop over in New
  York City for lunch with a friend?)
- advertisements and signs
- group discussion
- skits
- music, radio, television, film strips, slides
- writing exercises
- reading
- culture [81]

SUMMARY

In this and the previous chapters I have outlined the theoretical
and methodological background for the ACT Approach. Some of the guiding assumptions that have been derived from contemporary brain research,
from the work of Lozanov and the linguistic theories of Krashen and
others are:

→ We have extraordinary learning capacities waiting to
  be tapped.

→ An optimal learning environment is rich with multi-
  sensory, comprehensibly contextualized input and is
  not artificially or logically sequenced.

→ Among our most valuable resources are those that are
  subconscious.

→ Realizing our fullest potential involves tapping into
  and cooperating with our subconscious resources.

→ Suggestion is an effective tool for mobilizing our
  subconscious resources.

→ A relaxed, low-threat, low-stress environment is optimal for learning.

CHAPTER 4

THE A C T MODEL OF ACCELERATVE, FULL-SPECTRUM LEARNING

Overview

● **Accelerative, Full-Spectrum Learning is:**
- The result of tapping the remarkable reserve capacities of the brain.
- Learning which is more effectively retained.
- A relaxed, non-stressful experience.
- Playful, imaginative and enjoyable.
- Learning at 3 to 5 times the traditional pace.

● **Key Principles:**
- We all have extraordinary, unused potential.
- The optimal learning environment is relaxed and non-stressful.
- The mind creates its own "reality" on the basis of what it imagines to be true.
- We are all in varying degrees limited and conditioned by the beliefs we hold about ourselves, others and the world.

- The medium is inseparable from the message: as teachers we are embodiers, vehicles, channels for what we communicate.
- Teachers either serve to reinforce or help students transcend self-limiting attitudes and beliefs.

- **The Optimal Learning Environment is Characterized by:**

  - An artful teacher whose personal style is congruent and integrated with the purpose of the learning situation.
  - Multi-modal, multi-sensory, multi-plane experiences.
  - Lots of play!
  - Humor.
  - Fantasy and imagination.
  - Positively suggestive language.
  - Positive, supportive group dynamics.
  - Authentic communication situations.

- **Specific Means:**

  - Congruent, integrated physical environment.
  - Relaxation techniques.
  - Visualization techniques.
  - Metaphorical stories.
  - Music.
  - Games and role play.
  - Integrated peripheral stimuli.
  - Global, high-input presentations.
  - Supportive and integrated evaluation techniques.
  - Carefully integrated texts and materials.

Bridging Conscious and Subconscious Elements

My early training as a teacher had little to do with "teaching" and much to do with mastering content. I began my first classes as a teacher of German language and literature well prepared with information, rules, vocabulary, historical facts, etc., ready to begin a process which I conceived to be entirely conscious. I spoke to my students directly, asking for and expecting their interest and attention. When some of them showed little interest in German grammar or in the ideas of the German Enlightenment, I tried everything I could think of to engage that interest: I asked them questions, I drilled the grammatical exercises with even more fervor, I assigned compositions, gave quizzes and tests. I often succeeded in engaging their attention, but there was all too often an accompanying spirit of reluctant effort and duty. As the course wore on, energies seemed to flag, interest waned, and I felt compelled to work all the harder in an effort to hold students' conscious attention.

Looking back nearly 20 years later, I consider my efforts with a good bit of compassion, acknowledging my good intentions and recognizing a misplaced focus. I had been trying to work exclusively at the conscious level. That was the only way I knew how to work. That was where most of my teachers had "taught" me, so I thought. Consciousness, conscious mastery, conscious discrimination were the truly worthy objectives of an educated individual. This I believed, unconsciously echoing the biases of my conditioning. Although my own later psychological studies (Jung, Assagioli, Maslow) convinced me that the domain of the subconscious was a powerful personality component, I did not yet conceive of the implications of subconscious "reality" for classroom education. I still viewed the classroom as a place where consciousness reigned supreme.

Now, however, in the wake of such pioneers as Lozanov, Hart, and Krashen, a new awareness concerning the role of the subconscious in all learning and performance is beginning to manifest. A March, 1984 New York Times article entitled "Unconscious Unmasked as Major Pilot," begins with the lead sentence: "Suddenly, psychology is excited again about the unconscious." As contemporary researchers explore the frontier of how the brain functions, there is, the author states, "new and compelling evidence that the unconscious is the site of a far larger portion of mental life than even Freud envisioned." The new research is documenting that "the unconscious mind may understand and respond to meaning, form emotional responses and guide most actions, largely independent of conscious awareness." Emmanuel Donchin, director of the Laboratory for Cognitive Psychophysiology at the University of Illinois is quoted saying:

> An enormous portion of cognitive activity is non-conscious. . . .
> Figuratively speaking, it could be 99 percent; we probably will never know precisely how much is outside awareness.

One of the ways to tap those vast non-conscious resources productively is the skillful use of suggestion.

The Role of Suggestion

Of all the factors in the ACT Approach utilized to orchestrate an optimal learning environment *suggestion* is the most important, because suggestion is such a powerful tool to help students transcend their limiting self-concepts, beliefs and fears. And, in the case of most students, these internal limiters more than anything else prevent them from more fully realizing their learning capacity. Just as these self-limiting beliefs owe their power to their subconscious hold, so the positive power of suggestion is largely due to the influence it can have on our subconscious. As research has shown, if subconsciously we feel safe, confident, attracted, interested and playful within a learning environment, we will learn more rapidly and effectively.[82]

We all come to a new learning environment with expectations, assumptions, and beliefs which limit our capacity for experience in varying degrees. Lozanov quickly discovered that for optimal learning to occur, more than "positive suggestion" is needed. Students are not blank slates awaiting input. They enter the classroom highly conditioned by past environmental influences. They have rooted beliefs about themselves as learners, about their teachers, and about the learning process in general. Hart describes this situation in terms of the "biases" or the differing value-tones which are attached to all past experience. He speaks about changing the "biases" (in the sense of a + or - electrical charge) which permeate a student's stored experiences.[83] He writes: "all current learning is heavily influenced by previous learning. . . and by a vast array of stored biases," and "to change behavior, the biases must be changed, not the behavior directly."[84]

Lozanov, too, speaks repeatedly of the need to assist students to transcend their limitations, and he stresses the need for the de-suggestive / suggestive process which can help students replace limiting images and attitudes with liberating ones.

Fear is doubtless one of the greatest challenges that both teachers and students constantly confront in the educational process--a process which is, after all, one of growth and change. Fear is the hidden source and support of many of our most strongly held beliefs. Beliefs keep us safe and keep doubt at bay. To have them challenged is to encounter fear and the possibility of becoming disoriented and rudderless. Our fears serve to bind us to beliefs and behavior patterns which belong to the past and are not creative outgrowths of the "now." Our beliefs and fears have a determining influence on how we teach and learn. My own years of classroom experience provide potent testimony to this idea.

Twenty years ago when I was fresh out of graduate school, I taught language classes conventionally, using the audio-lingual approach in vogue at the time. I did not know any better and simply followed the model of my own teachers, who also had not known any better. I was anxious to succeed, anxious to appear competent and afraid to challenge the basic assumptions underlying the teaching of my mentors, my colleagues and myself. I did my best to represent the belief system which held that language learning required lots of effort, lots of homework, and lots of conscious drilling. I introduced dialogues, drilled them and followed the book's exercises and grammar presentations. I then tested, graded, and drilled all the harder. My classes were intense and demanding, and some students who could withstand the pace "learned" a lot of (about) German (in Krashen's learning vs. acquisition sense). I was an energetic, committed teacher/taskmaster, yet there was little joy and exhilaration in evidence – in me or my students. My prevailing attitude was one I had myself used: work hard now; great effort, even drudgery might be required, but the rewards could come after three or four semesters, when the basics are mastered. I was very skeptical about any method or approach which seemed to ignore the hard work that language learning appeared to demand.

Fifteen years later, thanks to a continuing personal quest and some wonderful, liberating teacher-guides, my teaching bears almost no resemblance to its beginnings. It has developed away from a set of survival behaviors veneered with confidence and institutional authority. It has become a way of life which involves continuing change, confrontation of fears and limiting beliefs, risk-taking, creative experimentation, playful classroom behavior and a great deal of joy. Fifteen years ago I did not dare "play" in class. I would never have dreamed of bringing a hand puppet into a college or an adult-education class (as I now do regularly). I would have been self-conscious, too afraid of looking foolish, afraid of insulting adult students, afraid of not appearing serious enough about teaching German. *Afraid* is the key word, and it was fear and its ally, ignorance, which prevented me from tapping more of both my own potential and that of my students. As soon as I became willing to begin abandoning my fears, my playful, intuitive and spontaneous resources emerged more freely, and the same types of changes began to occur in my students. If I am believable and fully present in my invitation to join in imaginative, playful communication, students feel freer to risk their own first steps in response. And once those first steps have been taken safely, once students see that everyone else is coming forward, too, the flow of motivated, willing energy has begun, and the crucial barrier reef has been passed.

My own teaching experiences have proven to me that as teachers, who we "are" (the beliefs and attitudes we are identified with) is inextricably intertwined with what we teach. We suggest and communicate through a myriad of ways to our students who we are and what we believe--about ourselves, about them and about what we are teaching. Our students, in turn, begin to reflect back to us the images we project upon them.

Two key areas, loaded with potent suggestion, and which teachers can learn to control significantly, are:

- The physical environment (which we, the teachers, usually inherit).

- The psychological environment (which we, the teachers, create).

The Role of the Physical Environment

The physical environment of an ACT Approach class is, to the extent possible, aesthetically pleasant, attractive, colorful, comfortable, and engaging to the senses.

- The lighting is, if possible, full-spectrum rather than fluorescent.[85]

- The predominant color is a subtle green with yellow, orange and blue used as highlight colors.[86]

- The floor is carpeted, softening the acoustics as well as providing an important comfort factor when games are played and students kneel, sit or lie on the floor.

- The walls have pictures, maps, and posters which are changed regularly to accompany the course content in an integrated way. These peripheral stimuli are aesthetic and relaxing as well as instructional.

- There are living plants and/or freshly cut flowers.

- Students sit in comfortable chairs which offer support for the arms and head, rather than using conventional desks.

- The room is well ventilated, has windows and plenty of natural light.

- Easels, flipcharts and/or white boards with color markers are used rather than a chalkboard.

- There is a stereo music system in the room to provide the various kinds of music used in the ACT Approach.

The reason for the departure of some of the above specifications from the norm of most drab institutional settings is as much psychological as physiological. In the ACT model, the teacher constantly strives to suggest the possibility of a new and different learning experience both qualitatively as well as quantitatively. We use every device to help students disassociate themselves from past, self-limiting attitudes toward learning, in order to serve the goal of liberating more of the student's potential.

The Role of the Teacher

The physical environment is certainly an important contributor to the psychological environment, but it is the teacher who most profoundly affects the suggestive atmosphere of a class. <u>Every teacher is an active and potent carrier of suggestion</u>--whether s/he is conscious of that fact or not. The ACT teacher becomes highly sensitive to this fact, so that his/her impact may become consciously purposeful and constructive. Let us note that we may now be emerging from a type of scientific educational experimentation emphasizing rigorous experimental controls which attempt to exclude "subjective" factors (such as the "teacher"). Previously, we believed these paradigms necessary to measure what "objectively" happens using a certain method. Now investigators within the scientific community are beginning to acknowledge the essential, critically important <u>and</u> desirable ingredient of subjective factors (persons, teachers, researchers.) It seldom makes sense to speak of a method (the "what") without the teacher (the "how").

Even before Lozanov's work, Rosenthal, documenting the "Pygmalion" effect, provided us with the startling evidence of how we as teachers can largely and unconsciously <u>determine</u> success or failure in our students.[87] We teachers have been invested with great authority: our voices, our eyes, our facial expression, our body language, our enthusiasm or boredom, our capacity to foster an engaging atmosphere (or its opposite), our encouraging attitude or our withering critical mien, our joy or our mechanical routine. The messages contained in such unconscious forces can literally create success or failure in our classroom. To become aware of the tremendous power we individually possess and to take proper responsibility for it challenges deeply yet provides a wonderful opportunity. Recognizing, strengthening and further developing <u>ourselves</u> as the prime carriers of the essential stimuli for success becomes a major area of continuing development for the teacher using the ACT Approach.

The ACT Approach uses a broad range of techniques drawn from many sources--but ACT emphasizes the "how" more than "what". This shift of emphasis is a challenge for many teachers, since they have usually been encouraged to think in terms of methods and techniques rather than in terms of cultivating in themselves *a way of being*. Fortunately, most teachers I have worked with find that the opportunity to go beyond techniques and to connect with both pedagogical and personal purpose is quite exciting and validating--of themselves and their career choice.

In sum, the ACT Approach teacher strives to create an atmosphere which is characterized by the following qualities:

- thorough competence in subject area
- genuine teacher enthusiasm for subject matter
- an atmosphere filled with a caring attitude, where fear is absent
- genuine teacher interest in and concern for students
- individualized appreciation for each student
- natural sense of authority and self-esteem
- mutual respect between teacher and student
- easy, relaxed teacher-student rapport
- skillful fostering of positive group dynamics
- playful atmosphere
- humor

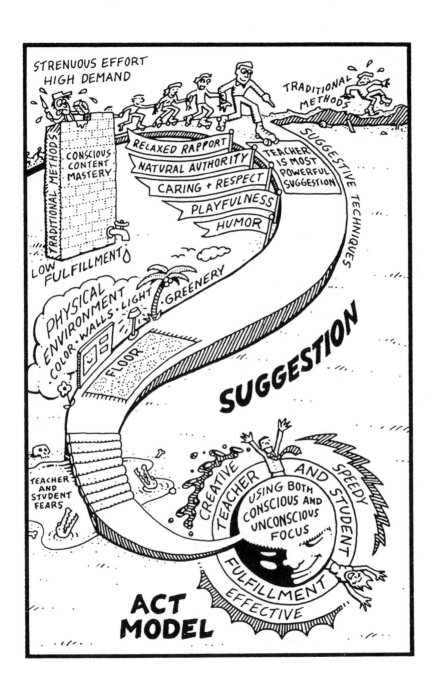

CHAPTER 5

SOME "HOW-TO'S" OF SUGGESTION

Excellent teachers, using whatever approach, will assuredly embody many of the positively suggestive qualities described in the preceding chapter. They do so naturally and largely unconsciously. The same qualities, which seem to be "natural" in some, can become more potent tools for effective teaching once we understand how to align them more congruently with our own objectives, and how to use them more consciously, skillfully and purposefully. Some ways we can use to develop these areas are:

Meditation and / or Centering Techniques

The use of meditative or centering techniques to help ourselves and our students become fully present for the experience of "now" can be a powerful suggestive tool. I take a few minutes alone before class to center my energies, letting go of distracting issues and thoughts, becoming as present as possible to the moment at hand. Often I do the same thing together with students as a group at the beginning of class, guiding a relaxation fantasy, loading it with positive images and affirmative suggestions. This serves to help the entire group gather its energies for the purpose of being together in a more fully present state of being. One possible example among many follows:

> Let's take a moment to gather our energies and become more fully pre-
> sent ...As you allow your breath to become deeper you will experience
> increasing relaxation and steadiness ...With each in-breath a wave of
> relaxing, calming energy flows in to quiet any tensions and discomforts
> ....Any thoughts or distracting concerns pass right on by, and you feel
> calmly alert and fully present, ready to experience and respond with
> your full self ...

There are many useful books on the subject of centering, meditation and imaging, and several are listed in the bibliography.[88]

Visualization Techniques

Visualization techniques can help us and our students identify and clarify purposes and objectives. Before beginning a course and also before beginning each class, I take a few minutes to sit quietly and visualize myself (in my imagination) as vividly as possible just as I would like to be in class, doing specific things, embodying certain qualities (such as caring, support, joy, delight, humor), interacting in specific ways with certain students (e.g. receptively, openly, supportively, firmly, authoritatively but caringly.)

I frequently guide students through a similar visualization process, encouraging them to see themselves learning and expressing just as they would most like to be able to do. This can be done effectively at the beginning of a class, before a test, in fact, before almost any task. An example which I often use at the beginning of a course is:

> As you relax, allow your imagination to help you recall a full and
> satisfying learning experience...it may have occurred recently or long
> ago, alone or with others .. a time when you learned something
> important to you ...Recall the setting. ..What do you see?...What do you
> hear?...What do you feel?....What special qualities does the experience
> have? (curiosity? joy? confidence? delight? etc.)....Allow yourself to re-
> experience those qualities, let them fill you....And now, as you gradually
> shift back to the present moment, allow the positive qualities of your
> special learning experience to remain alive within you and serve as
> resources which you can draw on as you open yourself to the day before
> you...

I have learned that the effectiveness of these guided visualizations depends every bit as much on my timing and intonation as on my choice of words. I find it very helpful to become an active listener to myself, becoming at some level a listening participant in the visualization. As I do this I feel much more aligned and congruent with what I am doing. I feel immediately more relaxed myself, and I sense a deepened rapport with the students.

Rapport-Building Techniques

It is extremely important for the teacher to cultivate and maximally use a positive "presence" in class. Building on inner preparedness as described in points 1 and 2 above, we can as teachers choose to be an increasingly available presence for students throughout a class. By *presence* I mean *a way of being*, with which the student senses rapport, trust, and ease. Rapport skills are crucial for effective teaching. Among the most effective strategies for me are:

- **Acknowledging Eyes:**

    As I began to pay more attention to my "suggestive" behavior, I noticed how often, (in my haste or busy distractedness), I would make fleeting or only perfunctory eye contact with those around me. What a difference it began to make as I began choosing to meet my students more authentically with my eyes--in such a way so as to say: "I really see you and am not in a rush to move on." I am not speaking of a penetrating look, or one which demands or asks anything or tarries uncomfortably long, but a seeing which is at ease, relaxed, accepting--simply acknowledging the person as he or she is. Just taking a few moments as a class begins to make acknowledging eye contact with all students in a class is a kind of gathering welcome and invitation which helps build good rapport.

- **Voice Intonation:**

    Just as we can acknowledge and almost embrace others with our eyes, so we can do the same with the quality of our voices. Our voice intonation says much that is deeper than the words we speak. Voice tone is largely expressed and received subconsciously. As we become more conscious of our behavior we can begin to align this powerful vehicle of suggestive expression with our best intentions. In my experience it has had a very positive effect on my students. After preparing myself inwardly as described in 1 and 2 above, I walk into class greeting students individually (as is practically appropriate) in a tone which expresses the pleasure I am having in seeing them and in being there to begin the class. Of course, it is counterproductive to feign such pleasure, since the students will almost surely detect the falseness, at least subconsciously. Thus, the importance of the preceding inner preparation.

My voice intonation continues to be a remarkably clear window into my inner state, attitudes and values throughout the class. If I am truly aligned with my best intentions and purposes, my voice intonation will express this alignment. Students will be much more likely to trust me and will be more and more willing to give assent to active, engaged participation in whatever "activities" I may have planned.

• **Body Presence:**

Our physical presence in the classroom projects countless messages, in a language our students understand fluently, albeit largely unconsciously. Learning to say with our bodies what we truly wish to communicate, i.e. aligning our physical expression with our real purposes has a very positive effect on both ourselves and our students. In my first course using the ACT Approach every class was videotaped. It was my first experience in seeing myself approximately as others see me. It was a revelation.

At first I was very critical of all my idiosyncrasies and unnecessary mannerisms. I noticed that the range of my body movements was quite limited. I tended to stand or move in a small area and gesticulate with my hands and forearms, often punctuating points I would make with a pointing index finger. However, as I continued to study the tapes I became more compassionate with myself and saw that my growing consciousness was providing a wonderful opportunity to change and to learn to express myself more fully and purposefully in a physical sense. In order to understand the effects of such a movement repertory, I watched the tapes with the sound turned off. My physical "language" seemed rather impoverished and, at times, dryly aggressive. I asked myself the questions: 1) how would I like to be? and 2) what would be appropriate and purposeful in this teaching context? I began some visualization work (as described in 2 above), some risk-taking in class--trying out some new movement behavior, such as allowing my body to align itself with the changing shades of enthusiasm in my voice tone. I began allowing more of my theatrical impulses, opening my arm movements so that they gestured invitationally instead of protectively, and so forth. One result was certain: I began to enjoy myself much more in the classroom. I know that if I am enjoying myself, the chances are that my students will enjoy themselves more. What comes across on the videotapes I see of myself now is a "me" that is much less reserved, more naturally expressive, and, I believe, more authentic.

- **Entrainment: Our Intimate Dance of Communication**

We all have times in our classes when everything seems to go just right. We feel understood, we feel connected to the other person and what they are saying. We feel comfortable physically, alert and alive mentally and at ease emotionally. Things just seem to click.

And, conversely, there are other classes where we feel out of sync. The topic of communication may be fine, but something feels off. We are just not on the same wave length with our students.

These two extremes of rapport (or lack of it) occur not just in our classrooms, of course--just think of the friend with whom you have that special connection, or the colleague with whom everything seems to be out of sync. Not to mention our children, parents, siblings, grandparents, employers, etc.

What is going on in our communication that creates such different feelings and experiences? A part of the answer lies in the subtle, largely sub-conscious physical changes we are experiencing and revealing as we communicate, or in what is known as "entrainment": the extremely subtle <u>physiological</u> echoing we do when we interact with another person.

I initially became acquainted with the idea of physical "mirroring" through NLP (Neuro-Lingusitic Programming). I began to notice how people in communication tend to "mirror" each other in crossing/uncrossing their legs and arms, tilting their bodies, and taking other matching postures. In fact, a good way to get into rapport with others, I discovered, is to deliberately mirror their body language--subtly, of course.

Then I came upon the research on "entrainment" by communication specialists William Condon,[89] Laurence Wylie[90] and Carolyn Fidelman.[91] I was flabbergasted by the degree to which <u>all</u> communicators do an unbelievably intimate physio–logical dance when we are interacting with another person. I first became aware of the phenomenon of entrainment when I watched a videotaped unrehearsed conversation between two native French speakers transferred onto a laser-disk. The disk slowed down the facial and body movements ten times or more without losing image sharpness.[92] From the instant when the speakers first greeted each other, their very different bodies, personalities and cultural styles began to adjust to each other. One girl was smoking a cigarette; her conversation partner was not. The smoker lifted the cigarette to her lips for a puff, and within a split second, the other girl lifted her arm to scratch her neck in a gesture which strikingly mirrored the smoker, only without a cigarette.

This "interactional synchrony"--another term for "entrainment" -- did not stop at the level of large movements of the limbs. Even more striking examples could be observed in a person's unconscious facial micro-movements. Close-up shots of each speaker's face, simultaneously shown on split-screen video, made it possible to observe very subtle expression changes. I was amazed to watch how nearly all speakers mirrored each other with their eye blinks, something that would go entirely unnoticed at the conscious level. Physiologically, we do not need to blink more than every couple of minutes, yet the speakers I was watching would often answer each other's blinks within 1/30th of a second! --totally out of the range of their conscious responses. Similarly, smiles and related mouth changes were also mirrored in split second fashion.

Condon notes that

> speakers' bodies move in precise synchrony with the articulatory structure of their own speech. The listener's body also frequency-modulates, at least within 50 milliseconds, to the incoming sound structure of the speaker's speech.[93]

Wylie elaborates:

> It is an astounding fact . . . that when two or more individuals are communicating, their body movements are locked into synchrony

with each other. Though silent, the listener moves some part or parts of his body precisely in rhythm with the voice and body movement of the speaker. There seems to be joint entrainment linking the two bodies during communication, even though this shared activity is out of our awareness. . . the more complete the interactional synchrony, the deeper and more thorough the bonding (i.e., of course, communication) between them.[94]

With such a deeply involved dance going on, is it any wonder that we feel very different in different communicational interactions? It really is like dancing with different people. We feel good, in step and in rhythm dancing with some people and not with others.

One of the striking implications of entrainment research is the realization that we communicate with our whole physiological beings, not just by talking. As Wylie asserts: "Communication is a synchronized interpersonal dance."[95] With some people we feel at ease and really get into the dance. With others we and/or our students feel "jerked around" or "stepped on." Listening to our bodies can help us become aware of when we are in sync and when we are in resistance. Tuning in to our bodies can give us the cue as to when something is "off" in our interactions and offer us the chance to make a shift which can make the "dance" easier.

An important awareness from these observations is that we are constantly inviting our students and others to do our dance with us at very subtle levels of interaction. If we are coming from an egocentric place, or are holding ourselves back, manipulating, etc., we are making it hard for another person to "dance" freely with us. When the "dance" is flowing well, it is probably a sign that we are in good rapport, entraining deeply, giving, taking, and exchanging messages at many subtle micro levels of synchrony.

The lesson for me of this research into entrainment has been the realization that I, especially with my body, am setting the tone and creating the atmosphere for what happens in my class. The metaphor of the dance has been helpful. When I ask myself, "Would my students probably like to join me in the dance I am leading now?" the answer is almost always useful. It raises my consciousness and gives me more choices.

In short, our bodies, our posture, even our tiniest movements, are powerful carriers of suggestion. All play crucial parts in the magnificent communicative instrument which we are. We can get to know these aspects of our own communication better and learn how to guide them into more and more purposeful alignment with who and how we want to be as individuals and teachers.

How we dress is a related point. Our clothing, grooming, and ornamentation speak volumes. Most of us are closely identified with the image we attempt to project through our external appearance. There is, of course, no "right" way to dress and groom as teachers--but clothing and appearance are important vehicles we can use to serve (or detract from) our purposes as teachers. Guidelines which have been helpful to me are:

- Since I wish to be perceived by the students as a thoroughly competent, trustworthy authority, and

- Since I wish to enjoy an easy, emotional and intellectual rapport with students,

- I will adjust my dress and appearance so that it is about one level more "dressed up" than the group of students I am with--not so much as to set me sharply apart--but enough to support comfortably my leadership role.

- Furthermore, I attempt to dress and groom myself in a way which will reflect the inner state I wish to project--without calling for others to notice me.

In sum:

> *The success of my lesson plan has at least as much or more to do with the rapport and atmosphere I am able to foster as with the specific activities planned.*

What may fall flat on one occasion may be splendidly successful on another, and the most important difference may well be how I *am*.

CHAPTER 6

THE EVOCATIVE POWER OF WORDS
Speaking to the Whole Person

In this chapter we will survey briefly some of the purposeful ways for a teacher to use language. Words are the main currency of our trade as language teachers, and the value of that currency depends on the quality of its "reserves." The yield of our language currency depends in many ways upon the skill with which it is invested. We will consider first the nature of a word's impact; then, some different categories of words and their effects; and finally, the metaphorical power of words. We will draw generously from the pioneering work done in this area by Milton Erickson and the developers of Neuro-Linguistic Programming (NLP).[96]

Words as Catalysts

When we communicate with another person using words, we evoke in that person internal representations associated with the words we use. When we speak the same language, we assume that the other person's representation is similar to our own, since without such similarity, communication would be nearly impossible. However, we may often forget that the difference between individuals in their own personal, experiential representations is likely to be greater than we assume.[97]

Spoken or written words function as triggers for internal processes in other persons. When I say "elephant," an English speaker will automatically make an internal representation of an elephant. This representation is influenced by an individual's composite life experiences with "elephant" and the associations accompanying the written or spoken word. Indeed, retrieval of "elephant" will occur even if we say: do not imagine an elephant.

Try the following: "Do not imagine a pink panther!" As you probably discovered, it is not possible to make sense out of my words without making some internal representation of them.

The important lesson in this for us teachers is to become aware of the evocative power of words. Our words trigger internal experiences and referents, which may significantly affect a student's performance and behavior in class. Thus, if my intention is to create a relaxed, non-stressful environment in the classroom, the many ways I may express myself verbally can either serve or detract from my purpose. Compare the following two statements:

- Welcome! I am delighted to begin sharing with you a new approach to learning which is fun, relaxed, playful and effective. In this class you will naturally and easily begin tapping into the extraordinary capacities we all have and find that positive learning is relaxed and pleasant.

- I would like to begin now, class. My name is Professor Schmidt. I hope you will enjoy this class. You don't need to be nervous or anxious about learning in this course. Forget your tensions and don't worry about trying hard. In this class we will go beyond our old limitations and leave behind our negative attitudes toward learning.

To make sense out of these introductory statements, a student must access his/her internal representations of the above words (which, of course, are tied to past experiences). Compare the following lists, derived from the two above statements, keeping in mind that each word is a catalyst for an internal process. Just what, specifically, that process will be for each student, we may not know, but we can meaningfully speculate about the general effect each statement will tend to make:

Welcome!	I would like to begin...
delighted	Professor
sharing with you	hope....enjoy
new	need
fun	nervous
relaxed	anxious
naturally	forget
effective	tensions
tapping into	worry
extraordinary capacities	trying
we all have	we will go beyond
find	old
positive	limitations
relaxed	leave behind
pleasant	negative attitudes

Although the intention may have been identical in both statements, the effect of each might be quite different. In the first remarks, the words trigger access to consistently positive areas of represented experience. In the second, the student will have to access non-positive representations repeatedly. Such images are likely to be incongruent with the quality of experience I wish to facilitate as a teacher.

In sum, awareness and attention to the evocative power of our words, how they can support or undermine our pedagogical purposes, can enhance the power of the messages we convey.

Words for Seeing *and* Hearing *and* Feeling

When we represent our experience internally, we do it in one or more of the following representational systems: visual, auditory, kinesthetic, gustatory, olfactory. Most of us have a preferred modality for representing our experience. Some of us are visually oriented and wish to *see* things "clearly." Others need to *hear* it, say it to themselves, and others convert experience into *feelings* and *tactile* representations. Very few represent experience primarily in the modalities of taste and smell, but these senses are also powerful triggers for calling up certain experiences.

As a teacher, if I happen to represent most of my experience visually, a visual focus will reflect itself in the language I use, particularly in the predicates. I might typically speak to the class in the following way while guiding a fantasy:

Good morning! As we begin to relax today, *picture* yourself in a comfortable place. See if you can *focus clearly* on the *scene* you are in. It may be *dark* or *bright*, in *black* or *white*. As you look around, you will begin gaining *perspective* ....

Or, if I were predominantly an auditory person, I might speak as follows:

Good morning! As we begin to relax today, *listen* to my *voice speaking* to you and allow the *sounds* to *hush* any *dissonances* which may be disturbing an inner *silence*. Just allow my *utterances* to remain in *earshot*. They will not be too *loud* , and the *tone* of my *voice* will *ring quietly* in your *ears* , promoting general relaxation...

Or, if I were predominantly a kinesthetically oriented person, I might speak as follows:

Good morning! As we begin to relax today, *feel* all the *tension flowing* out. *Feel* all the *stress float* away. And you begin to get *in touch* with a *gentle warmth spreading* throughout your *body* . Your hands are *hanging limply* at your sides, *holding* onto nothing....

Each of these guided fantasies might have been effective for some students--especially for those who shared the same representational tendencies. For them, I would be providing the most natural, easy access to the state I am wishing to lead them to. For others, however, I may make it unnecessarily difficult by unwittingly calling for experience consistent with my preferred modality rather than theirs.

When we are communicating with one or two other individuals, we can, as skillful communicators, match our language with theirs, in the interest of facilitating rapport and easier, more effective communication. When teaching in a group situation, individual matching is usually not practical, but we can consciously learn to use a balanced language, which offers all students, regardless of their modality preference, opportunities to resonate with our language and establish rapport. An example might be:

Good morning! As we begin to relax today, just *listen* to the regular *tone* of my *voice* and *feel* any *tension* begin to *flow* out of your body. *Picture* yourself in very calm surroundings, and allow your *eyes* to move gently over the *scene* of your choice. *Listen* for the natural *sounds* which accompany this setting. *Feel* the agreeable *temperature* and *textures* around you and enjoy the *feeling* of *ease* and *comfort* while being here.

The following list of predicates may serve as a reference for guiding the choice of language according to the particular purpose:

Visual Predicates	Auditory Predicates	Kinesthetic Predicates
blackness	call	bind
bright	click	break
clear	clash	cold
colorful	crashing	cool
enlighten	discuss	dig
focus	harmony	feel
fuzzy	hear	firm
glimpse	hum	float
grey	listen	freeze
hazy	loud	handle
imagine	mellow	grip
inspect	noisy	grasp
ogle	quiet	hurt
paint	roar	nail
peek	scream	painful
perspective	shout	pounding
picture	silent	pressure
pretty	sing	push
preview	screeching	rough
see	squeal	scratch
seem	talk	solid
sketch	tinkling	squeeze
show	thunderous	stretch
vivid	told	unravel
watch	tune, tune up	warm
witness	yell	wring[99]

The Use of Metaphors

Metaphors can be a powerful tool in tapping the suggestive power of language. Metaphors and images are a primary communicative means of the subconscious. As we learn to communicate more effectively on that level with our students, we can better facilitate tapping the potential which resides there. Used purposefully, metaphors can greatly assist our students in transforming the beliefs and self-images which may be limiting them.

Using metaphors to respond creatively to problems--in the form of stories, jokes, parables, fairy tales--has been a form favored by teachers (often wise) since time immemorial. All the major religious traditions have made use of the metaphorical story to communicate their teachings. Metaphors appeal to multiple levels within us simultaneously. They are frequently able to bypass or penetrate the set attitudes, categories and limitations of the conscious mind. Speaking the language of the subconscious, the metaphorical story can provide parallels to our own life situations as well as universal patterns of behavior, joy, suffering, and conflict, offering resolutions which resonate meaningfully and acceptably with the inner experience and personality structure of the listener.

Stories not only entertain; they can also alter our experience so as to facilitate growth and change. The use and/or interpretation of metaphor has become a standard therapeutic strategy for counsellors and psychotherapists and a fine art among the best of them. To name but two of the finest, Carl Jung and Milton Erickson have contributed models for both understanding and working transformationally with symbolic and metaphoric communication.[100]

With some study and practice, the FL (or other) teacher can hone his already considerable skill in using metaphors and acquire additional technical sophistication. Beginning to guide relaxation and imagery experiences is a good way to begin.[101] An excellent resource for the art of constructing metaphorical stories designed to encourage therapeutic change is David Gordon's *Therapeutic Metaphors*.[102] In addition, the communications model known as Neuro-Linguistic Programming (NLP) is a valuable source of guidance for improving the purposeful use of metaphorical communication.[103]

Two examples of how metaphorical communication are used in the ACT class follow.

• A Guided Fantasy Recalling A Positive Learning Experience

I use the following guided fantasy on the first day of class. I regularly precede it by a guided relaxation similar to the one combined here.

As you begin to collect your energies. . . . and become more and more present. . . . you can notice the regularity of your breathing, . . . allowing it to be as comfortable, slow and deep as feels good. . . . If it feels more comfortable. . . . to close your eyes. . . . that is fine. . . . And as you become aware. . . . of the chair supporting your body....securely and easily....you can let any discomfort go....as if it were flowing. . . . right out through the chair.....These special chairs. . . . have been provided. . . . so that . . . . it is easy to relax. . . .The support for your head. . . . encourages you to relax. . . . your neck, your head and mind. . . .The support. . . for your arms. . . allows you. . to rest your arms . . . and open easily. . . to new experience. . . . The pleasant colors . . . and objects in the room . . . invite you to enjoy yourself. . . through your senses.. . . . . . And as you relax deeper and deeper . . . . you may find it easy. . . to drift back to a time. . . when you learned something new, . . . when learning filled you. . . with joy and satisfaction. . . . A time when you experienced. . . that learning is easy. . . and as natural. . . as breathing in .... and breathing out. . . . This special, positive. . . learning experience . . . may have occurred recently . . . or months or years ago. . . . You may have been alone,. . . with a friend,. . . a teacher, . . .a guide. . . you will remember. . . .And as you re-experience. . .re-live this special,. . . positive learning, . . .you may hear all the sounds. . . that are there, ... smell the fragrances. . . .see all the details of the scene. . . . feel the positive sensations. . . accompanying the experience. . . . You may even . . become aware. . . of the essence of this experience . . .which makes it so special. . . .It may be wonder,. . . delight,. . joy,. . .mastery,. . . self-appreciation,. . . excitement,. . . confidence,. . . or another quality. . . .you will know. . . . Whatever that essence is, . . . you will be able . . . to let it begin filling you now, ...so that the essence . . . of this special learning experience. . . resonates throughout your being. . . . reminding you. . . that this experience . . .is a resource for you,. . a valuable possession. . . which you can call upon. . . to remind you. . . how you love to learn, . . .how you are able . . .to learn naturally, . . .easily and successfully. . . . You may even realize . . .that as you embark . . .upon new learning experiences, . . .all you have to do . . . is recall your positive learning experience, . . . and your mind will become attuned. . . to the way. . . you like to learn,. . . attuned to the way . . . you learn effectively and successfully. . . . And in the days and weeks ahead, . . . as we help each other . . . enjoy learning together, . . . you may find . . . that there is some part of you, . . . some inner sign which awakens . . . when it is reminded . . . of your special experience . . . .and you may find . . . that the special essence. . . will begin to emerge . . . again and

*again . . . to help you experience . . . the kind of learning . . .you are seeking.
. . . . . . In a minute. . . we will be returning. . . with our conscious awareness
. . . back to this moment, . . . to this room, . . . and when we do, . . .you will
find it easy . . . to bring with you . . . some of the essence . . .of your special,
positive learning. . . . You will feel refreshed,. . . alert . . . and awake, . . .
ready to utilize . . . your inner resources . . . and the resources of the group
. . . and this class . . . to full advantage. . . . Now, in your own time, . . . at
your own pace, ...slowly bring your awareness back here, . . . to this room,
. . . together with the other people here. . . . . As you open your eyes, . . .
notice the objects and people around you. . . Listen to the sounds in the room.
. . . feel the firm floor beneath your feet. . . . . Welcome back. . . I sense . .
. that that was a special experience for some of you. . . . I trust . . . that it is
a positive way to begin our learning adventure together. . . . .*

Commentary:

• Tempo in Guiding Fantasies

The tempo is slow and relaxed. The conscious mind tends to be in a
hurry. It may well become bored with the fantasy. That is fine. The
subconscious mind is the one we are primarily speaking to here. The spaced
periods in the above text indicate regular, rhythmical pauses. This can
assist in the deepening of the relaxation process. Students' breathing will
tend to synchronize to the rhythmical delivery. The rapport tends to
become deep and the suggestions will be more evocative and effective.

• Degree of Directiveness

When guiding fantasies such as the one above, much of the
metaphorical or imagistic content will be provided by the student. In
general, guided fantasies are most effective when they are not over-
directive. The details, when left to the experiencer to provide, will
generally be more powerful. An exception to this are guided fantasies used
to review language content. In that case, the teacher provides a wealth of
detail and vocabulary woven together with interesting images. For the
student these images can be like going to the movies--and understanding
the soundtrack in the target language!

• Embedded Suggestions

One of the powerful suggestive tools of linguistic communication is
the use of embedded suggestions. Few people enjoy being told what to do.
Many individuals react negatively to overt authority and have developed
a kind of reflex resistance to verbal commands. An effective way to

circumvent resistance to positive suggestions which are actually intended to help students successfully access their own learning potentials is to embed suggestions within certain linguistic structures. Used in such a way, positive suggestive images can by-pass the conscious mind, eluding detection by resistance mechanisms. Suggestions can be marked out vocally in such a way as to be perceived and accepted by the subconscious mind. More than 20 such suggestions are contained in the above guided fantasy. As a demonstration of how such forms may be experienced, I would ask the reader, before reading the next paragraph, to read aloud in a normal fashion the first five lines of the above guided fantasy.

Now, after having read those lines normally, read the following underlined phrases from the same text, in isolation:

As you begin to collect your energies and become more and more present you can notice the regularity of your breathing, allowing it to be as comfortable, slow and deep as feels good . . . .If it feels more comfortable to close your eyes, . . .that is fine . . .

Through subtle changes in pitch, intonation, or directional projection of the underlined phrases, it is possible to "mark" them out in such a way that they are consistently communicated in a characteristic way, unnoticed by the conscious mind but perceived and possibly accepted at the subconscious level.

• Embedding Direct Suggestions:

Another suggestive technique used in this fantasy is the embedding of direct suggestions, e.g. " ... when *learning filled you with joy and satisfaction ...* " or "*a time when you experienced that learning is easy and as natural as breathing in ... and out ....*" Note that in this last example the technique of abruptly changing verb tense from a past association to the immediate present may serve to intensify the experience and draw the listener more deeply into the immediacy of the moment.

• Anchoring:

A further, powerful suggestive tool is to intonationally "mark" certain words or phrases as "anchors" for later re-association. Anchoring is an associational strategy used extensively in NLP. "An anchor is any stimulus that evokes a consistent response pattern from a person."[104] Any sensory modality may be used, but for the teaching context auditory/verbal anchors are most practical. In the above guided fantasy the teacher could consistently "mark" out the words "special, positive learning experience" with a perceptible shift in intonation. It is important to use an intonation which is distinctively different from the one normally used in regular speaking. Otherwise, at some other time, the teacher might inadvertently "call up" the anchor without any intention or purpose. This might not have any particular adverse effect, but indiscriminate word choices could weaken the continuing associational strength of the anchor. In using these techniques, I time the first special intonation as exactly as possible with the moment when I judge that most students are fully experiencing their recalled experience of positive learning. I reinforce the association several times more during the recall experience.

The process of anchoring is designed to deliberately associate a stimulus to a particular experience. If the timing is good, so that the "anchoring" association coincides with the fully evoked experience, the anchor will "take," and the next time the anchor/stimulus is used, the associated experience will be accessed. When the anchoring process has been skillfully executed the stimulus/response mechanism can be called upon to serve the learning process on later occasions.

For instance the first week of the course provides a valuable opportunity to root as deeply as possible the students' positive associations to learning a FL in this class. Having anchored on the first day the experience of a highly positive learning in the student's past, I can evoke the recall of the essence of that experience by using the phrase "special, positive learning experience" with the same perceivable intonation I used to mark it on during the guided fantasy on the first day – without having to repeat the entire process. For example, I might begin the second or third day with a short relaxation before commencing some communicative activities. As a part of the guided relaxation I might say:

And. . . as you continue to relax, . . . you may begin to look forward . . . to the special . . . positive . . . learning experiences ahead. . . .

Anchoring, as most of the other suggestive techniques discussed, require practice and consistency. I have found it helpful to begin experimenting on a modest level, perhaps marking a phrase one day, making a note of it, and then repeating it in a purposeful context, with the same intonation for several days thereafter. Experience builds confidence, and with each step accomplished, it becomes easier to stretch ourselves toward a new growth point.

Story as Metaphor

The following story might be used effectively more than once in a course. For example, I might tell the story in English during the first few days of class. Later, I might retell it in the target language toward the end of the course. The first telling would be meant to reinforce the rapport- and confidence-building suggestions given during the first days of class. The later re-telling in the new language would help students bridge their learning experience forward into the future.

There is the story of a young woman, Christina, who leaves the home of her parents in order to make her way in the world. She is seeking to go beyond the over-familiar routine of her family and take on the challenge of the new and untried. Christina travels to the Uni-Center of Growth and Wisdom, a special place cherished by seekers of all kinds, located in the heart of the land known as Namreg. She arrives in the fall, just as the leaves of the trees are beginning to change to colors of deep red, orange and yellow, and the trees are preparing to turn to their life within. Christina is somewhat anxious because she has never been to Namreg and does not understand the language spoken there. When she arrives and hears people speaking so rapidly in such unfamiliar ways, she feels afraid and wonders if she might have made a mistake in coming here. It was so easy to understand her friends back home, and the distance between her ignorance and the others she sees in the Uni-Center makes her doubt her decision. There are other learners here from far away besides herself, but they don't appear to be afraid.

Then, as her doubt is beginning to grow, she meets one of the guides who welcome the new seekers and help them begin their course of initiation in the Uni-Center. The guide's name is Karelov. Karelov is a kind, gentle man who greets her in her native tongue, and yet soon has her feeling comfortable listening to his native Namreg. She is amazed at how relaxed and confident she feels with her guide. Her understanding of what he tells her grows quickly, and before long she is beginning to respond back in Namreg. Karelov sees that Christina has all the abilities she needs. With his insight, support and encouragement she begins to open her mind and heart to the opportunities around her. Karelov spends many hours with Christina and a small group of seekers. He tells many stories, plays delightful and fascinating games with them, and listens with patience and interest. They all learn rapidly, scarcely realizing it is happening.

Christina's confidence grows quickly. She begins to speak to other seekers, to laugh, play, and joke with them. She looks forward to her regular meetings with them and Karelov. She recognizes that their challenges, fears, strengths, and hopes are similar to her own, and the warm bonds of friendship begin to deepen.

One of these friends, Bruno, invites her to the annual festival dance in Namreg. Karelov has taught them the traditional dance forms of Namreg, and they demonstrate their skills with ease and delight at the festival occasion. There are not many seekers at the dance who are as inexperienced as Christina and Bruno, and many of the natives come to them and congratulate them on their naturalness and ease in expressing themselves in such new forms.

During one of the intermissions, one of the traditional dance instructors of the town by the name of Pedantaway asks them how many hours and days they must have drilled for such a performance. How surprised he is when they respond that they never drilled, but just danced for fun to Karelov's music and imaginative descriptions. The dance instructor cannot believe it and suspects they must be lying. Christina and Bruno become a little confused and wonder if they may have done something wrong. They cannot understand all this fuss, all these questions, all this analysis of what had just come naturally.

Just at this moment, Karelov and his partner, Bellissa, who are also attending the dance, gracefully come up to Christina and Bruno and invite them to join in a dance for four. The young pair tell Karelov of the incident with the dance instructor, and Karelov smiles. He explains that the Uni-Center is not free of those who get stuck in outworn beliefs about how learning must occur. Many still cannot accept that mastery can come without strenuous, forced effort. Pedantaway may have forgotten that play and natural spontaneity release our best capacities to learn. Christina and Bruno realize from their own recent experiences that what Karelov is saying is true, and as their friend and teacher offers his hands for a new round of the dance, a smile of recognition appears on the young couple's faces. In an instant they are again dancing freely, naturally, with skill and delight.

The next day Karelov announces to Christina, Bruno and the rest of the group that their initiation orientation is complete. Their comfort and competence in understanding and speaking Namreg is fully adequate to proceed on their continuing quest. They have all mastered naturally and with ease the basic skills necessary for what is ahead. Their understanding and vision of themselves and others has grown, as has their confidence and self-appreciation. The friendships will continue, the pleasant memories will remain, and the ending is but a beginning.. . . .And with these words Karelov opens his arms, inviting all these friends to join in the great circle dance of strength and unity.

Christina has since become a fine teacher herself. Bruno has become a master of Namreg communication. They and their friends continue their quests, without haste, following easily and naturally the best guide of all--the Karelov who resides within.

Commentary

The purpose of the above story is to provide students with a positive, supportive metaphor for their own experience as learners. The metaphorical quality of this story is rather obvious and would probably be perceived by a number of the students. This is not necessarily good or bad. For students who are consciously resistant to learning, the more subtle and indirect the metaphor, the more likely its acceptance. For most students, however, more fearful of failure and lacking in confidence, such a story can be effective at both conscious and unconscious levels.

A well constructed metaphor is as "isomorphic" (structurally parallel) to the listener's situation as possible. When working with individuals one can, of course, tailor a metaphor to a more detailed degree than when working with groups. In the above example, certain situational elements characterizing the beginning FL student's situation were assumed:

- Students' past experiences have been highly conditioned. They are partly aware of this fact. Coming to the university is probably part of an effort to transcend the limits of their conditioning.

- Coming to the university and to a FL class is on some level connected to a deeper personal quest of the student toward meaning, success, fulfillment.

- The challenge of learning a new language (perhaps even of attending the university) is anxiety-producing. There will be feelings of doubt and of "I can't."

- The helpful guide/teacher can provide an environment in which student fears will disappear and their natural abilities will be affirmed and fostered.

- Students will encounter teachers and others who will insist on the prevailing socio-cultural norm that learning is difficult and requires strenuous conscious effort.

While the metaphorical story acknowledged the above factors, the following suggestive elements were built into the metaphor to suggest alternatives and possible resolutions.

- **Pacing:** Pacing, a term from NLP, describes the variety of things one can do to demonstrate to another person that one is "acknowledging" his situation, is "with him," is "hearing" or "understanding" him, "seeing" where he is coming from. Pacing is used to establish rapport. In the above story the entire first paragraph has a pacing function. It is designed to mirror metaphorically the general situation of most students in my beginning FL class.

• **Leading:** Once rapport is established the next step is to initiate movement away from the problem state toward the desired state. In the above story this function is embodied by the guide Karelov. He meets the students where they are and gently guides them away from their doubts and fears, toward an appreciation of their capacities, through a natural learning process, toward their goal. He is a metaphor for the ideal teacher.

• **Positively suggestive language and images:** from the second paragraph the vocabulary of confidence, ease, opening up, naturalness, success, play, enjoyment dominate the descriptions.

• **Positive inter-personal relations and group interaction:** paragraphs three and seven give expression to the positive effects of supportive group interaction and inter-personal bonding. Positive group dynamics is an essential ingredient for the success of an ACT class.

• **Overcoming renewed doubt and challenge:** students who learn a FL through an acquisition rather than a conscious learning approach often become natural targets for those favoring conscious learning. The challenge in the above story is presented in the form of a pedantic dance instructor who wishes to explain the naturally and subconsciously acquired competence of Christina and Bruno in conscious, analytical terms. Students with acquired competence may not be prepared to defend or explain what they do naturally, without thinking. The understanding and authority of their guide/teacher is designed to give them the trust and confidence they need to affirm their experience when faced with inner and/or outer challenges.

• **Future pacing:** future pacing (another NLP term) involves bridging to the future. Once the problem state (such as tedious learning) has been successfully worked through using metaphors, images of possible, successful future applications or expressions are suggested. Here, the career manifestations of Christina and Bruno, as well as the allusions to the continuing growth of the group as a whole, locate the positive, successful experience of the story in a plausible future, with which the student may choose to identify.

- **Name symbolism:**

  ‣ Karelov is a combined play on the words care and love.
  ‣ Namreg is German in reverse
  ‣ Pedantaway is a play on words, i.e.: away with pedants.
  ‣ Christina and Bruno are typical German names, easy
      for beginning students to identify with.
  ‣ Uni-Center is a play on University.

<u>In sum</u>:

    Pacing establishes rapport with the listener's present state; leading involves transformational work, in this case using a metaphorical story to mirror a transformational growth process toward a desired outcome; future pacing bridges the inner (transformational) experiences to possible expressions in the external world. In addition, the story provides abundant opportunities for embedding positive suggestions, suggestive play on words, and evocative imagery. The entire process is designed to appeal to the subconscious mind, and to access its potential for acquisition of a new communication system.

CHAPTER 7

GETTING STARTED RIGHT
Crucial First Impressions

Lozanov argues that the inner set-up of the learner--his beliefs, attitudes and prejudices, are limiting factors which must be "de-suggested" if a breakthrough to his greater potential is to be achieved. As commonplace as the knowledge is that first impressions are important, we teachers, (with the captive audiences we are generally assured), often miss the opportunity to capitalize on our first contact with students. The first contact sets the stage for what can follow.

Setting the Stage: Before the Course Begins

The suggestive / desuggestive process actually begins even before the first class. The process begins with the student's expectations. Some of the factors which contribute to a student's expectations about a class are:

- his attitude toward himself as a learner
- his attitude toward teachers and school
- opinions of his peers
- course description in catalog, flyers, bulletin, etc.
- teacher's reputation
- school's reputation

At first we might think that we have no influence on a student's expectations before we ever meet him. However, it is often possible to influence some of the above factors which contribute to the formation of a student's crucial inner set-up--even before the course begins. Although to influence the school's reputation or even one's own may take a long period of time, we can usually have some degree of influence on the last four factors. It is effective and relatively easy, for example, to affect the first contacts with written announcements about our courses. Several ways of doing this are:

- Create a lively brochure and/or flyer about the course and make it available to students (bulletin boards, registration tables, enclosure in general school mailings, etc.) This can be done, no matter what educational level you work in.

- Suggest an interview and/or feature article in the school paper about the course, the approach, the innovative ideas, etc.

- Write a letter to each student who pre-enrolls in your course (or as soon as you have a class roster), welcoming him personally to the class. Express your own goals and describe some of what you plan. I have been told repeatedly how much students enjoyed receiving a _personal_ invitation to a class and that it very much influenced their positive expectations about the class.

The First Day of Class

The first day of class is the most important day for the ACT Approach. This is when first impressions are being made, attitudes and beliefs are being confirmed or modified, expectations raised or lowered. Such processes go on to some degree all the time, but it is in the opening moments when conditioned attitudes will be most amenable to change, since reality has not yet completely confirmed them. Once they are set, the experiences to follow are likely to become variations on fixed attitudes, unconsciously locked away out of reach of most conscious attempts teachers use to motivate students.

As an M.D. and psychiatrist, Lozanov was very aware of the powerful effect the first consultation can have on patients. Positive suggestions coming from an authority to a receptive patient can have a dramatic "healing" effect which reach far beyond whatever physiological problems might be involved. His further work with suggestion indicated that the teacher can have a parallel effect in helping students with their disease in learning. At the outset, if a student suspends his/her self-limiting inner "set-up," s/he can begin to open to experience a positive alternative to past perceived possibilities. Suspended beliefs are the beginning of the type of liberating change envisioned in the ACT Approach.

The following paragraphs outline some ways of maximizing the positive and potentially liberating impact of the first class:

• The Room

▸ General Arrangement:

The room can be a strikingly pleasant place to enter: attractively arranged, comfortable chairs in crescent formation, colorful fabrics on floors and walls, interesting and visually engaging pictures and posters; ample but comfortable lighting; music playing in the background. In short, as a student walks in for the first time, s/he is not greeted by "more of the same" but rather is pleasantly and invitingly alerted to fresh, new possibilities.

▸ Purposeful Use of Visual and Peripheral Stimuli:

Lozanov's research documents remarkable learning results using visual stimuli integrated into the instructional environment without the instructor drawing conscious attention to them.[105]

Dr. Lawrence Hall of Howard University has reported using these techniques to teach the Russian Cyrillic alphabet to students in just a few hours.[106] I have not attempted to document the effectiveness of such techniques, but I am convinced by evidence that at a semi-conscious level the peripheral visual environment is absorbed in minute detail.

If we are able to integrate linguistic content with visual images, thereby weaving stimuli together which stimulate both hemispheres of the brain for active decoding, we will have enhanced and enriched the instructional environment. Thus, I create posters which blend language paradigms with decorative visual shapes (circles, arabesques), balanced in different colors. Attractive, aesthetically pleasing ethnic landscapes and cultural scenes surround language information posters. Such peripheral visual stimuli, however delightful and noticeable, once perceived, cognized and ordered at some level of the brain, begin to lose intensity and impact. Thus, the images need to be revitalized, recast or transformed, in order to remain stimulating. I rearrange and/or replace the pictures and posters and other visual objects about every three days, as a way of keeping the room visually alive and intriguing.

We can allow the room to make its own impact, before we appear. When my students arrive on the first day, there is hot water in a corner for coffee or tea; relaxing music is playing; comfortable chairs await them, and they can take a seat and absorb the unexpectedly pleasant atmosphere for five or ten minutes before I enter.

▸ Student Seating

Another way to maintain a lively, varied set of stimuli is to change students' perspectives by altering expected seating patterns. If the room and number of students permit, crescent seating patterns are far more preferable to conventional row blocks. When students are looking at each other, seeing faces and real expressions, they are much more likely to engage in real communication with each other. The conventional classroom arrangement focuses attention on the teacher and on the chalkboard. It is highly desirable to use seating patterns which encourage student-to-student as well as student-to-teacher interactions.

In addition, where a student sits affects his/her experience quite significantly. It will also affect how we as teachers interact with him/her, and it can either contribute to fixed expectations or help transcend them. All teachers experience how students (like everyone else) are habitual about taking the same seat every day for the entire course. This is a lamentable and unnecessary fixation.

"Fluid seating" is an effective strategy containing implications for the student's visual experience as well as group dynamics and the general climate of change and interesting novelty. From the second hour on I ask students to choose a different seat each time they enter the room. I explain how the room will look different depending on the particular angle of perspective, and how the group dynamics will remain livelier and more interesting as we discover new neighbors and new faces across the room. Fluid seating is another technique of the suggestive / de-suggestive process which can help students find fresh, unconditioned experience, leaving old limiting patterns behind.

• First Contact

When I first enter and make contact with students, I am ready to give my full attention to the experience. I make it a point not to fuss with papers, folders, books, chalk board, and so forth. I am fully there with them and for them. I have taken time to center and prepare myself inwardly and my body language, facial expressions and voice tone all communicate the message that I am glad to be there, that I am prepared to be there, am confident, and am also sensitive to their situation.

• Non-Verbal Messages

I am generous with easy eye contact which intends to include and invite. I am thoroughly enjoying what I am doing and believe this attitude communicates itself in countless ways. I am clearly interested in sharing my enjoyment with the students. Such non-verbal messages are powerful and quite disarming for most students. Many students come well-defended with strategies about how to survive the authority and demands of a teacher. These unspoken messages encourage students to suspend old judgment patterns and join in the fun, at least as long as it seems safe.

Keeping it safe is absolutely essential. Suspending old attitudes and beliefs is risky business until a safe alternative has been found--an alternative that can be trusted. Thus, in the beginning the students may respond with an often wary, provisional acceptance of what is going on. That is fine. Trust is made solid through time-tested experience.

• Opening Welcome

I welcome the students both verbally and non-verbally. I express my pleasure at having the opportunity to engage with them in the unique learning adventure which lies ahead, and I proceed to outline in broad strokes the novel and liberating assumptions upon which the course is based. I explain the exciting results they can expect to achieve--not on the condition that they work hard--but by virtue of their innate capacities to learn, which can and most certainly will be tapped in this process, a process which has succeeded with many previous students just like themselves.

• Grades and Dispelling Fear of Failure

After suggesting the images of success and enjoyment, I outline the simple requirements and grading policy for the course. Students are assured a passing grade if they attend regularly. (The grade options and policy is fully described later in Chapter 13.) Thus, in a matter of minutes, one of the greatest barriers to learning, fear of failure, has been dealt with. Students are then able to give themselves fully to the experiences to come without repeatedly needing to calculate a possible grading consequence.

• Invitation into a New Language

With this beginning, the stage is now set to commence. I begin by sharing briefly with the class why I love German and why I love to teach it. I also mention how much all of them have already been affected by persons who experienced the world through the medium of German (Einstein, Mozart, Freud, Marx, Hesse, Jung, etc.--as well as Hitler), and how enlarging and exciting it can be to open a window onto other worlds for ourselves as well. I then invite students to relax into their chairs and listen to some "word-music" with me, just as an experience in sound. I recite a short poem by Rainer Maria Rilke and invite students to share the response it evokes in them. After several recitations I ask them to fantasize what these words might be attempting to communicate. It is always remarkable how much students are able to glean just on the basis of intonational patterns and cadences. I use this experience to point out how fluent they are already in many universals of language, and that they will be able to build on their solid grounding in language per se as they become fluent in German.

• Invitation to Play: Assuming a Fantasy Identity

The introduction is designed to provide a very positive first encounter listening and hearing German. The students are then invited to begin with me the adventure of discovering and acquiring this new language. To do this, I explain, it is easiest and most enjoyable to proceed in an imaginative and playful spirit. We learn best when we are mentally relaxed, and we are dynamically relaxed when at play. An easy way to play is to pretend that we are someone different than we "really" are. I then invite them to playfully embark upon this group adventure by assuming a new name and life-role which can provide the basis for much fun and imaginative development. One or two large posters colorfully display German names. I read the names with considerable variety of intonational expression, asking students to imagine being christened Ingrid, Hans, Else, Udo, etc., and to "feel out" which name they would like to assume. The choice of a new name provides magical moments. I savor these with the students, expressing my delight with their choice, repeating the name, allowing time for it to resonate and be fully acknowledged. The smile of delight lights up a face as a person takes a new name. Their assent to play as they call to another by new names, becomes powerful, positive rapport-building experience for students of all ages and backgrounds.

‣ A New "Profession" or Life Role

In addition to choosing a new name, students are invited to fill out their new identity with an interesting new role to play. A list of "professions" or "roles" is presented on colorful charts. Sample professions are dancer, lawyer, adventurer, pilot, ne'er-do-well, monk, secret agent, millionaire, king, wise woman, etc.

A very effective touch when students select their profession is to offer them a "prop" to accompany their choice: a crown for the king, a wad of paper money for the millionaire, a pair of dancing shoes for the dancer, a picture of his/her Mercedes to the obviously rich lawyer, etc. Rummage sales, costume stores, etc. are good sources for props. Another excellent source is to ask the students themselves to come next class with a prop they would like to have help symbolize their new life role.

‣ The "Cocktail Party"

The climax of this opportunity for personality transformation is a noisy cocktail party, replete with imaginary champagne, where students make the rounds introducing themselves in German, using a <u>very</u> brief cocktail party style:

● Guten Tag! Ich bin . . . (Hans)! *[Hello! I'm (Hans)!]*
■ Guten Tag! Ich bin . . . (Ingrid)! *[Hello! I'm (Ingrid)!]*
● Freut mich, Ingrid! *[Pleased to meet you, Ingrid!]*
  Ich bin . . . (Fußballspieler)! *[I'm a soccer player!]*
■ Fantastisch! Ich bin Zigeunerin! *[Fantastic! I'm a gypsy!]*
● Sehr interressant! *[Very interesting!]*
■ Auf Wiedersehen! *[Good bye!]*
● Auf Wiedersehen! *[Good bye!]*

Offering students the opportunity to assume a new identity is a simple device, one which many FL teachers have used in differing approaches. New identities are a seemingly light, innocent and fun touch, yet the potential of this simple transformation is seldom realized or purposefully exploited by teachers. It remains too often a nice touch for only the first day of class, or is used by the teacher but never taken up by the students themselves.

The power of this technique lies in the student's acceptance of a new image and his/her consent to actively play. As mentioned earlier, the ACT Approach strives to promote disidentification from self-limiting beliefs and images. Used skillfully, offering to students a new fantasy identity, including a new name and life-role, can have an amazing liberating result. Students are given permission to play "as if," and if the teacher can skillfully model and support a relaxed, playful atmosphere, students will respond in remarkable ways. Their ego-investment and limiting self-consciousness diminishes, and spontaneity and humor begin to to take their place.

The fruits of such an "identity change" become increasingly apparent as the students begin to embrace the fantasy, addressing each other in their new roles. Indeed, every time "Wolfgang" addresses "Udo" and the latter responds in kind, there is mutual assent to the "play" taking place. In an atmosphere of play we are naturally relaxed, alert and open--key ingredients for rapid, holistic learning.

However, like nearly all techniques, the success of taking a new identity lies more in the *how* than in the *what*. Offered mechanically or routinely, a new identity might be accepted dutifully and/or awkwardly. Offered with imagination and delight, a new name and life-role can be a doorway to new opportunities for freer self-expression, enhanced self-image and success. That such results should happen in a FL class is astounding (and freeing) to most students. The key lies in <u>how</u> the teacher offers and sustains the opportunity for transformation.

Before beginning the "cocktail party" described earlier, students are led through their first of many singing experiences. I introduce a boisterous "identity song" with a preposterously simple "melody": *Ich bin ich* (I am I, you are you, he is he, etc.) The song involves much pointing and laughing, and as a result, students quickly become comfortable in <u>playing</u> with the "I am," "You are," forms they will be using in the cocktail party.

These activities seem to violate one basic principle of the ACT Approach, that is, "comprehension before production." The reason for encouraging students to venture speech production within the first hour has to do with the group bonding process. This brief cocktail conversation occurs in a room noisily filled with other such conversations. No one is judging the quality of performance. There is much laughter, handshaking, even hugging, and accuracy is hardly a concern--rather, playful communication. This brief exchange, affirming as it does the newly assumed roles, playful interaction among students, verbal and non-verbal language, body language and body contact, is a wonderful rapport-building device, and sets the stage for many positive group interactions to come.

Language Through Actions: An Initial Semi-Silent Period

The rest of the first day is spent using variations on the Total Physical Response (TPR) approach developed by Asher.[107] These activities use variations on the imperative form in combination with physically acted out responses. In the early stages of language introduction, especially in the context of the positive group rapport established through the above steps, these activities work very well. The reader may consult publications by Asher, Segal, and Seely listed in the Bibliography for many helpful suggestions and a thorough practical and theoretical description of the TPR approach.

In earlier variants of the ACT Approach, prior to spring, 1983, I followed Lozanov's practice of introducing the first large block of new material through the concert sessions on the first day, following the "cocktail party." Although I (and others) have had excellent results using that sequence, I now choose to anchor the student's quickly growing self-confidence and listening comprehension skill through TPR and other communication activities before exposing the student to the written language or the expressive speaking demands required by the new language. In German the interference resulting from the associations to English lexical combinations is a considerable obstacle for many students and may become an unnecessary and undesirable complication during the first few days. I now postpone the first concert presentations of material until after 10-15 hours of TPR and other listening comprehension activities.

Among proponents of approaches which focus on developing communicative competence, there is general agreement that it is a mistake to encourage speech production before laying a solid groundwork in listening comprehension skills. Krashen states that "we acquire spoken fluency not by practicing speaking but by understanding input, by listening and reading,"[108] and he considers "that forcing early production, before the student has built up enough competence through comprehensible input, is perhaps the single most anxiety-provoking thing about language classes!"[109] Asher, in his Total Physical Response Approach, recommends an initial silent period of approximately 10-20 classroom hours.[110] Krashen offers the simple advice that "a safe procedure is simply not to force production and let the student decide when to start talking,"[111] and he cites the guidelines offered by Roger Brown to parents who wish to "teach" their children how

to talk quickly--guidelines which are highly relevant for the the FL
teacher:

> Believe that your child [read: "student"] can understand more than he or
> she can say, and seek, above all, to communicate. . . There is no set of
> rules of how to talk to a child [student] that can even approach what you
> unconsciously know. If you concentrate on communicating, everything
> else will follow.[112]

One general principle of the Natural Approach developed by
Terrell is that "production is allowed to emerge in stages."[113] Terrell understands "production" as "response by nonverbal communication" as well
as single word responses growing into combinations of words, to phrases, to
sentences and finally into more complex discourse.[114]

The ACT Approach is in agreement with the advocates of an initial silent period. This period is not designed as one where verbal responses are not permitted. However, during this time, students are allowed
to be actively silent, ingesting the rich offering of comprehensible input
provided in the first days of class. The students are largely silent, but they
are actively demonstrating their comprehension by moving, pointing,
shaking their heads, laughing, and soon are responding with single words
such as yes, no, here, there, you, me, he, she, it, etc. During this period,
there is no anxiety about correct production, about sounding silly, etc.
Student confidence builds very quickly, a playful spirit is easy to maintain, and the group bonding grows and deepens. The semi-silent period
yields especially valuable results when used in the ACT Approach, because the positive atmosphere is allowed to provide the climate for all
language activities.

This relatively silent period is a departure from Lozanov's pure
Suggestopedia. In that model, used in the first few courses I gave at the
University of Massachusetts at Boston, students are introduced to a large
volume of written material the first day. They begin oral elaborations on
this material the second day of class. I have experienced even better results by delaying the introduction of the text and the first invitations for
oral production (with the exception of the rapport-building activities outlined in the section on the first class) until approximately the tenth hour
of class.

CHAPTER 8

THE ACT TEXT

During the first 7-10 hours of class no formal text materials are used. Words, phrases, and diagrams are written or sketched on easel pads with colorful markers. Single sheets of illustrated conversational speech are used. Many pictures provide contextual clues for comprehension. Gradually, single sheets of illustrated vocabulary and phrases are given to students to supplement classroom activities.[115]

The "text" occupies a central place in nearly every approach. Even if the focus is on oral communication activities, there is usually a written set of materials which serve as the basis for elaboration, review, testing, etc. For the more recent "acquisition" models, text-dependency is not so complete, but written, illustrated materials are a valuable element in the instructional design. Although more conventional, commercial texts can be adapted for use in the ACT Approach, a specially written text is highly desirable. Its introduction and place in the course requires special consideration.

Main Features

Since suggestion plays such a central role in this approach, the text offers a great opportunity to combine language content with embedded suggestions at many levels designed to help students learn. The principles and practice outlined in the earlier section on the teacher's use of positively suggestive language in the classroom can be fully applied to the preparation of the written materials. Because of the unique manner in which the text is musically introduced to students who are in a deeply relaxed and receptive state (described in the next chapter), the many levels of messages carried by the text will have a greater impact than material studied in a conventional, consciously analytical manner. Specifically, the main features of a special ACT text are:

- The text introduces 1500-2000 new words for the 90-hour Level 1 course.

- The text is written as a series of approximately nine "Acts," compromising a coherent dramatic story with richly developed, authentic characters, situations and plot.

- The Acts are 500-700 words long; the first is the longest, introducing 500+ new words.

- The Acts are written in dialog format, in parallel columns, with the target language in the left column and the mother language equivalent in the right column.

- There is no formal sequencing of grammatical constructs, although earlier Acts are written with simpler, yet authentic, language. Basic grammatical structures and paradigms with examples are presented in appendices. They may be referenced by students as they acquire interest in forms and abstractions.

- The text is amply illustrated with images designed to suggest and reinforce the content being presented.

- On the left facing pages of the dramatic dialogs there may be sparing, often humorous explanatory glosses of words, phrases and forms which will facilitate comprehension and/or drawings, cartoons, images, photos to visually reinforce the suggestive purposes and to enhance interest.

- The text is not bound. It is held by attractive 3-ring binders in different colors. Because new material can be withheld, suspense and interest in Acts yet to come is heightened. Also it is possible to revise and supplement the text regularly.

- The text itself serves as a powerful vehicle for several different levels of suggestion:

‣ The appearance and format of the text have a suggestive impact. Students do not buy the text at a bookstore; they pay a "materials fee" for the course. Thus, at the appropriate moment, the instructor is able to "present" the students with an attractive, new text, guiding with suggestive principles in mind their first encounter with the written materials.

‣ Direct suggestion is used in the text. The introductory and instructional statements to students contain positive and encouraging suggestions to help evoke positive attitude and expectations. Such statements are written in a confident, personable, helpful tone, inviting students to make rapid learning advances by tapping resources they may not have used. Students are encouraged to enjoy the drama, participate playfully in it, and use it as a creative springboard to their own growing communicative style.

‣ Indirect suggestions are embedded throughout the text. Characters in the drama encounter similar challenges, obstacles and frustrations (both literally and metaphorically) as might be predicted for most students. The way the characters successfully handle situations, through their attitudes, their thoughts, their statements, is all being projected through the material, often in the form of compelling images directed at subconscious receptive levels.

For example, the main character in the first acts of the ACT German text is an eleven year old "Wunderkind," a delightful prodigy who wins the hearts of the adults he interacts with, as he playfully and humorously models the behavior of a free spirit who loves to live and learn. The entire first Act of the ACT German text is reproduced in Appendix 1.

Commercial Texts

Many commercial language texts today are increasingly "communication" oriented and often provide activities which can be useful. Such texts, however, are still substantially different from a "suggestopedic" text, which offers the richly suggestive dramatic dialogs for concert presentations. Presently, the best suggestopedic or accelerated learning texts available are parts of commercial packages designed primarily for independent, home use. As such they are, in my opinion, the best

independent way to begin acquiring a language. The best programs I am
aware of are those by PLS and those by Accelerated Learning Systems.
Their texts are attractive and imaginative, and the tapes are
incomparably superior to those in traditional approaches.

Supplementary Materials for Grammar and Practice

The ACT text is a lively drama, filled with key vocabulary and
situations for conversational re-enactment. It's rich and varied input parallels the language banquet offered by the acquisition-oriented teacher.
Its purpose is to aid "acquisition" more than "learning." "Learning," however, is an important component in the ACT Approach and is supported by
the use of supplementary materials which explain *about* the language
clearly and offer opportunity for some written practice. I have experimented with a number of more traditional texts as a reference and practice
source,[116] and have found that they can be used as helpful "learning" sup-
plements. The danger is to be lured by their authoratative structure and
drift into assigning and expecting more of them than is appropriate for an
acquistion-oriented approach. I assign short sections for grammar study
and practice nearly every day as a consciousness-raising experience. I do
not expect mastery. See Chapter 11 on the role of homework.

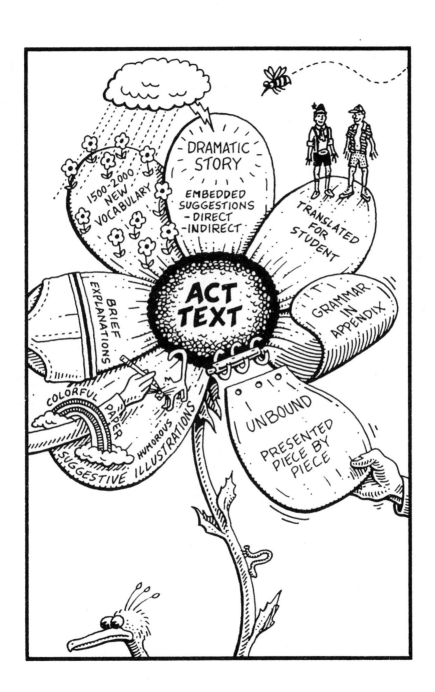

CHAPTER 9

MUSIC AND THE PRESENTATION OF MATERIAL

One of Lozanov's most original contributions is the role he assigns to music in the "concert presentations" of new material. The ACT Approach has incorporated this powerful technique and a description and discussion follow later in this chapter. Before that, however, some remarks on the role of music in general are in order.

The Role of Music

Music is one of the most potent carriers of suggestion operating in our culture. Nearly everyone in this age of radios, stereos, tape recorders, compact discs, etc. reaches frequently for music to accompany moments of his/her day. For many of our students music has become such an habitual accompaniment to the point that one could speak of dependency or addiction. It is outside the boundaries of this book to enter into a discussion of the merits of the various musical forms dominant in our culture today. It is common knowledge, however, that much of rock music popular with young people today is rife with suggestions of physical and sexual violence, escape into drugs, facile sensuality, and sex, as well as alienation and hopelessness. Music (and the powerful images which often accompany rock videos) has become one of the most powerful conditioning forces in our culture.

The question for me as a teacher has been: how can I use this powerful medium, to which my students are so sensitive, to pedagogical advantage? My answer has been a developing experimentation with a wide variety of music for different purposes.

In my first Lozanov-inspired courses, before the ACT Approach evolved, I used music as he did: exclusively for the "concert presentation" of new material. Having a stereo system in my classroom, however, soon led me to other uses.

• Background Music before Class and during Breaks

I sensed right away that music could help me establish the climate I wished to create. Students come to class with every conceivable inner mood and attitude. It is crucial for my goal to establish rapport and lead students to a highly resourceful state. Music can be of great assistance. Instead of a student being greeted by a silent space where his possible negative state could easily continue, he would hear the infectious upbeat sound of the Canadian Brass Ensemble playing Baroque fanfares or of one of Mozart's bright Divertimenti. In a matter of minutes I could watch the physiology of students change: more color in the face, brighter eyes, more outward posture. Much of my first task had been accomplished for me by the music.

• Background Support for Guided Fantasies and Relaxations

I soon discovered that certain music[117] enhanced the relaxed or fantasy-like atmosphere I was trying to create during guided fantasies and relaxations. After a few experiences students would begin to drop into deep, relaxed receptivity after a few seconds of such music.

• Songs: Folksongs, Popular Songs, Classical Art Songs, and Folkdances

I like to introduce a lot of songs without music--in my own groping way, looking for a key which I and hopefully others can manage. Such "creating it in the moment" has a fun, invitational quality which no polished recording can match. And, recordings bring in a wonderful dimension of variety and scope and standard. I use everything from German beer drinking songs to Marlene Dietrich to Lotta Lenya to Dietrich Fischer-Dieskau to Nena with "99 Luftballons." Not to mention folkdance music for in-class dances--a great energy raiser and group bonder. Once again, timing, purpose and the "how" are the decisive factors.

• General Background Music: To Use or Not to Use

I have had lively discussions with colleagues about the appropriateness of playing <u>any</u> kind of music as steady background. I inadvertently discovered that playing certain classical music in the background at a barely audible level during much of the class had a very positive effect--a rather startling discovery for me who has always disliked elevator and retail store "muzak." Indeed, as a trained musician, I had always found any background music distracting, since I tended to focus on listening to the music rather than on what was intended to be foreground. However, it was by forgetting to turn off the music after a break or after a guided fantasy that I discovered that the continuing background music had a positive effect. After ten to twenty minutes, when the tape would come to an end and shut off abruptly, a student would often suggest continuing the music. I, too, would then notice that the environment without the music was suddenly somehow "bare" and wanting to be filled out. Thus, I began to experiment with playing intentionally background classical music at a barely audible level and noticing how it helped group attunement and rapport, how it provided a cohesive element, noticeably lacking when it was not there. And I began to learn how to use it for my own pacing, learning to move, speak, bridge in subtle but significant relation to the music as I proceeded to guide the class.

I began exploring further in my teacher workshops the possible reason for the positive effect of background music. I would typically conduct the following exericise with my workshop participants: I play 3 to 4 minutes of Mozart's Divertimento for Strings, K.136--just as a listening experience. Then I ask participants to share the qualities they would attribute to the music they just heard. I have conducted this exercise with at least twenty groups of teachers of widely varying fields, from Germany, to America, to Brazil. The list of qualities always looks strikingly similar, typically including the following qualities:

vitality	energy
positive	optimistic
dramatic	lively
order	spontaneity
freedom	harmony
balance	humor
depth	joy
delight	playful
beautiful	imaginative

The next step is to ask oneself the question: "Would I like for *my* *class* to be characterized by these same qualities?" I have not yet had a participant who answered "no."

Playing Mozart's Divertimento will not, of course, automatically transform our classroom so that the above qualities describe it. The point is, however, that as Lozanov and others (particularly NLP practitioners) assert, we automatically and subconsciously begin to align and harmonize ourselves with the operating peripheral stimuli in the environment. If it is rock music, we may begin to twitch our bodies and move our feet. If it is bright light, we will probably begin to squint. If it is Mozart's Divertimento we will instinctively begin to adjust to the values that music embodies. My working hypothesis is: when I play this music at a low but just audible volume, the qualites such as spontaneity, vitality, order, balance, etc. are filling the acoustic environment of my classroom. These qualities are surrounding me and my students and we are subconsciously attuning ourselves to them. They provide an environment which positively interacts and supports other strategies I may use to achieve spontaneity, vitality, order, balance, etc.

I have no objective proof that my hypothesis is accurate, only my own subjective observations and those of many teachers who are using music similarly. The feedback I have gotten from teachers who are actively using background music as described above is nearly unanimous: the teachers feel supported by it in their instructional activities; the students like it and ask for more; students seem to be more relaxed and more cooperative.

The objections or reservations which various colleagues have raised have to do with the distraction which background music will cause and with the imposition of a "muzak-like" environment. The objections, I might add, have all come from teachers who have never tried using the music in the way described above.

I have had an occasional student who will complain in the first week of the music being a distraction. I will promptly reduce the volume and suggest to him that in a short time he will feel more comfortable with the low-level stimulus. I explain that the purpose of the music is to assist in creating a multi-modal, brain-compatible environment for enhanced learning, and that his feedback is important so that I can make an appropriate adjustment. It is important that the student feel heard and responded to. I have never had a student who continued over time to be bothered. (I make it a point to check with the student days later to see if the music is still a distraction.) To the second reservation I can only say that I do not play "canned," recipe-like "muzak," but rather fine performances of musical masterpieces with the purpose of providing a backdrop of highly desirable qualties to which I and my students may attune.

All the above uses of music enhance markedly the sensory variety and quality of my classes and provide a powerful right-hemisphere stimulus to interact with the verbal component. The most unique use of music in the ACT Approach, however, occurs in the "concert presentations" of new material described below.

The Presentation of New Material: Musical, Relaxed, Global, and Multi-Modal

The ACT Approach text contains the basic vocabulary content of the course, but it is not presented or utilized conventionally, but rather, it is introduced in a special manner. First, it is given in a global prelude-like form, and then in a unique synthesis with music. These techniques, developed by Lozanov, have potent suggestive as well as physiological impact and are congruent with the growing understanding of the human brain and how learning best occurs.

In our earlier discussion of the ideas of Hart, Lozanov and Krashen, we found that a large volume of input which is not artificially simplified or logically sequenced, is essential to a full-functioning, healthy brain. These researchers all recommend increasing the volume of real, multi-sensorial input by factors up to ten times what students presently receive.

The ACT Approach accomplishes this objective. The material to be learned is offered in a high-input, multi-sensorial and global presentation rather than in more traditional linear, logical dosages. Students are immediately offered a wealth of stimuli. The classroom itself is filled with a rich array of stimuli in a relaxed, inviting setting, from which students can begin forming patterns. Thus, they may unconsciously acquire a foundation for "understanding" before they hear a word in the new language, in fact, even before the teacher first enters the room. During class, there is almost constant input at sensory levels--things to hear, touch, see and smell. The text offers easily up to 10 times the amount of material conventionally introduced in foreign language texts.

To expect such a quantum leap would ordinarily strike fear into most students (as well as most teachers!). And fear is, as we have argued earlier, the single most debilitating factor in the educational experience. However, in the ACT Approach the leap is made without fuss, as it addresses this challenge better than perhaps any other known approach, by giving maximal attention to creating a non-stressful, fully supportive and positively suggestive environment.

• The Global Prelude

The first, more formal, "presentation" of text material, comes during the global prelude to the "concert session." Considerable linguistic material has, of course, already previously been introduced both through TPR techniques and through pictures and activities using the Natural Approach.[118] The global prelude has two purposes:

- ▶ to swiftly preview material and create a context for what is to follow
- ▶ to "suggest" indirectly to the student that what is coming is interesting, engaging, and comprehensible.

The global prelude may be described as follows:

The teacher begins by announcing with an attitude of interest and anticipation that a new textual unit is going to be introduced, mentioning that they (the students) will be able to understand it with ease. He then "enacts" the basic content of the new unit, using appropriate props (objects, costume articles, pictures, posters, etc.) and pantomime. There can be short, discursive asides and brief questions, but the atmosphere remains playful and the interest level high. One of the keys here is _interest_. As Krashen very persuasively argues:

> . . . the best input is so interesting and relevant that the acquirer may even "forget" that the message is encoded in a foreign language. . . It is very difficult to present and discuss topics of interest to a class of people whose goals, interests, and backgrounds differ from the teacher's and from each other's. . . [and] relevance and interest have not been widely perceived as requirements for input, since so many materials fail to meet this requirement.[119]

The task of creating genuinely interesting materials is of truly crucial importance, as is the task of creating the context where they can come to life. I am sure that we all have had the experience of the teacher who criticizes the "lousy" text he or she must use, joins in with the students in commiserating, and then justifies the poor results with more scapegoating of the text. It is of critical importance that teachers believe in the potential effectiveness of the materials they are using. Editing, adapting and supplementing may be necessary, but if the teacher has no respect or confidence in the materials, this attitude will be communicated to the students and will likely frustrate any attempt to stimulate their greater potential.

When the global prelude is effectively presented, the student experiences an intriguing performance where he is challenged in a non-threatening way to stretch her/his capacity to comprehend. And, as a consequence, the student succeeds, is able to follow, feels competent, increases her/his confidence and thus becomes interested and psychologically prepared to receive the large volume of content which will follow.

Peripheral aids in the room, without necessarily being consciously referred to, may also support the creation of a context for the unit to come. These may include posters with key phrases from the unit, colorfully written names and and key words from the unit, or even grammatical paradigms which will be exemplified in the unit.

Key to the effectiveness of the global prelude--as to the success of nearly every phase--is the *way* in which it is presented. If it is done routinely or mechanically, unit after unit, it may suggest the opposite of the desired intent. It needs to be delivered with genuine interest and delight, in the spirit of communicating something which the students will really enjoy learning about. Then, the atmosphere of authentic communication will be sparked, and the natural interest which accompanies it will further stimulate the learning process.

• The Concert Presentation

Along with his theory of suggestion and its impact on learning, another highly original methodological contribution of Lozanov is his use of music as a suggestive carrier. After experimenting with a variety of techniques to relax students and suggestively present new material,[120] Lozanov found certain kinds of music an ideal medium both for the purpose of creating a mentally relaxed state and for providing a vehicle to carry the material to be learned into the brain. He theorized that music, (which activates the right hemisphere of the brain) could be wedded with the word, (which activates primarily the left hemisphere), thus significantly facilitating the "encoding" of material in the brain in holistic learning process.[121] To accomplish this synergistic effect Lozanov conceived the "concert session," where large amounts of new material might be presented. The concert session contains two musical presentations of the same material, each using different music and a different communication style, as outlined below:

• The First or Active Concert

For this concert, music from the classical (1750 - 1825) and romantic (1825 - 1900) periods is used – by such classical composers as Haydn, Mozart and Beethoven, and such romantic composers as Brahms, Rachmaninoff and Tchaikovsky. I personally prefer to use the classical composers for the concert readings, since their music is both dramatic, emotionally engaging and ordered, harmoniously structured, ending in a balanced resolution. It stimulates, invites alertness, and its harmony and order evoke ease and relaxation.

The teacher delivers the new material in a specially intoned, dramatic fashion, guided by the music's tempo, dynamics, color, and phrasing. The teacher integrates him/herself as a special instrument with the other musical voices. The music is neither used nor experienced as background. Rather, the music is a fully active partner, with which the text is wedded, molded and woven together so that it is carried smoothly and as seamlessly as possible to the receptive learner.

The students silently follow this concert presentation, using the texts which they have been provided. The target language, which the teacher is reading, is printed in the left column, and the English equivalent is in the parallel right column. During the ample, frequent pauses in the reading, the student can readily glance at the right-hand column to check for the English equivalent, as needed.

Graphically, the first concert presentation may be represented as follows:

Voice:

Music:

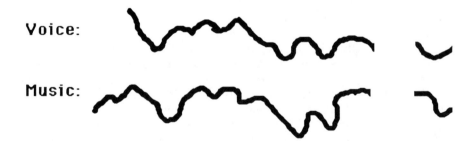

• The Second or Passive Concert

This "concert" presents the same material as the first concert but uses Baroque music (music composed from about 1600 to 1750), preferably the slow, largo movements.[122] The music of Bach, Händel, Vivaldi, Telemann, Corelli (among others) has a less personal, more rigorously structured quality than the later classical style, providing a background of order and regularity which supports very well the more straight-forward presentation of material during this phase. This time, the teacher reads the material naturally and idiomatically, guided not by the music but by the semantics and context of the text.

The students do not follow the second concert reading with their texts. Instead, they are invited to close their eyes and experience the easy flow and mixture of words and music. They need only listen, unconcerned about meaning or whether the text of the music seems to be foreground.

Graphically, the second concert presentation may be represented as follows:

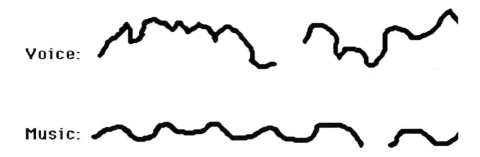

At the conclusion of the second concert, I allow the adagio music to continue playing for several minutes. This gives the experience a chance to "anchor" or sink in and facilitates a slow, gentle end to the class. There is no further discussion. Only a *"Das ist alles für heute. Auf Wiedersehen."* (That's all for today. Good Bye.)

The teacher treats the concert sessions with a certain degree of ritual, giving them a quality of heightened, suggestive expectancy. Lozanov asserts that the most important phase of the suggestopedic learning cycle, that of encoding the material in the brain, occurs during the concert presentations.[123]

The first concert lasts approximately 30 minutes; the second, 10 to 15 minutes. Concert sessions are offered about every eighth hour of the course. They are always structured to end that particular day's class.

The concert sessions complete the "formal" <u>receptive phase</u> of the ACT Approach. What follows is the <u>active phase</u>.

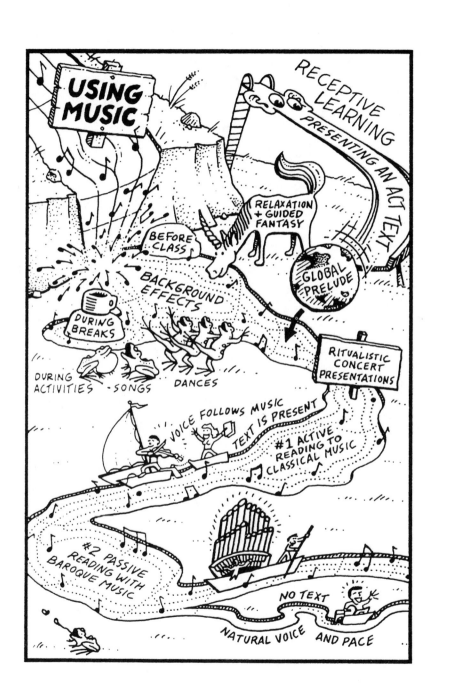

CHAPTER 10

THE ACTIVATION PHASES
Retrieving and Using What Is Learned

Activation Is More Than Speech Production

The expressive and receptive activation of presented material occurs almost constantly in many forms. Activation occurs as students listen and comprehend, or as they grasp the relation between a facial expression, body gesture, picture, voice intonation and language meaning. They constantly demonstrate their "active" comprehension when they respond to commands and requests, nod in agreement or disagreement, or display facially any number of other possible, appropriate responses.

Activation also means beginning to use expressively the speech patterns which have been heard, internalized, sorted, patterned, and associated. A guiding principle which the ACT Approach shares with both the Natural Approach and the Total Physical Response Approach is: Don't push students to speak! Evelina Gateva, Lozanov's master demonstration teacher, formulated this principle simply and directly: "Spontaneous, not early activation."[124]

Once the receptive/concert phase has been completed, the next step is to begin the process of receptively and expressively activating the previously encoded material. This involves finding a means to facilitate retrieval and natural ease in use. The activation phases in the ACT Approach have two main stages: primary and secondary, as described below.

Setting the Stage for Easy Activation

The primary activation session begins with the next class following the concert sessions. It is the students' first expressive engagement with the material. Before beginning this phase I always spend some time assuring good group rapport. Good activities for this are the sharing of humorous anecdotes, listening to a short song or poem, or most often, a visit by a puppet:

• Puppets and Rapport

Before beginning to use the ACT Approach, I had never had any experience with puppets and was afraid my students would think puppets were silly or might become insulted. Having seen Evelina Gateva use it successfully with the Lozanov method, I decided to risk bringing a puppet into class. Again, I am thankful I ventured into unfamiliar territory. I now regularly introduce "Onkel Fritz" after the first 3 to 6 hours of class, after my goals in group dynamics are well underway. By this time students are delighted to have some more fun as they learn. The puppet quickly becomes a further opportunity for the entire class to create spontaneous "happenings" in the realm of fantasy. As with students' acceptance of new class identities and names, their assent to interact with a puppet is assent to play "as if." Students are often able to communicate more freely with this humorous character than with a "real" person, especially since the "real" person happens to be the "teacher." Since by nature, a puppet represents a created imaginative character, it can provide an excellent role model for easy communication.

With the assent to play comes spontaneity and increasing abandon to the moment, an optimal climate for language acquisition and learning in general. My primary puppet, Onkel Fritz, quickly becomes a family member of the class, and interaction with him (all in German, of course) becomes the springboard for some especially effective communication activities. Onkel Fritz is a balding, 70 year-old Bavarian adventurer, who loves Schnapps and females and is convinced he is as young (at heart) as anyone. His engaging and humorous anecdotes and appeals for opinions and advice rapidly lay the groundwork for colorfully personal relationships with nearly everyone in the class.

For example, I created in Fritz a flirtatious bent that seems to produce an amazing variety of responses, from motherly reprimands and advice to brotherly alliances. One class consented to help him find a more permanent female partner, offered strategies, and suggested texts for a personal ad in the classifieds. Several days later a letter for him had been pushed under the door before class--from "Brunhilde." A new female admirer who had been inspired by his romantic ad.

Variations on puppet interactions are limited only by our imaginations. I have observed that imagination--both mine and my students'--seems to expand as steadily as does their communicative competence in a climate of playful risk-taking. Puppets stimulate the imaginative child in both students and teachers. This dimension, when purposefully integrated into our classes, can become one of our most valuable resources.

Primary Activation Activities

Although using a puppet more technically belongs to the category of "secondary activation," discussed later, a puppet is also highly effective in setting the stage for the "primary activation" of material. Once a light and comfortable atmosphere has been established, I can easily move to engage playfully with the material from the previous day's musical presentations. This primary activation of material typically uses several of the following strategies: 1) whole group choral echo/antics; 2) simultaneous role reading in diads or triads; 3) individual or small group role reading for the class with costume props; 4) comprehension check. These activities are used for a block of text approximately 250 words in length.

• Whole Group Choral Echo/Antics

This is usually the first activity I use with new textual material. I ask the group to stand with their texts in hand and echo my model reading of the text. (Having students stand frees their bodies for much more active involvement, and also facilitates fuller voice production.) I exhort them to echo and even exaggerate my dramatic intonation, to be loud and boisterous, above all <u>expressive</u>! I explain that the focus is on <u>playful, enjoyable interaction</u> with the text--not a drill. In addition I ask them to <u>imagine vividly the images</u> in the text as they speak and encourage them to find an <u>accompanying gesture</u> with their hands, arms, heads or bodies to go with the image in the text. I explain that by simultaneously and actively using our imaginations, the sound of our voices, the gestures of our bodies and an emotionally playful spirit, we are maximizing a range of learning styles and memory anchors. Such an explanation seems to help students more fully engage in the activity.

• Role Reading in Diads or Triads

I usually follow the above whole group choral work with a variation on the same material in diads or triads, depending on the the number of roles in that particular section of the text. (Note that since the ACT Text is written as a drama in dialog form, there are always character roles to interpret playfully and imaginatively.)

My instructions are to re-enact the dialog section as freely, expressively, and dramatically as possible. Students remain standing for this activity, but may sit and/or move depending on the action in the dialog.

• Individual or Small Group Role Reading for the Class with Costume Props

After the above energetic, playful and enjoyable engagement with the text, I often ask for volunteers to enact that section for the whole class. By this point students are so warmed and loosened up that there are always volunteers.

It is important to keep this activity playful and light. Costume props for role reading help keep the focus off the "real" personality of the reader. Hats of all kinds, glasses, jewelry, jackets, aprons--much of it brought in by the students themselves--quickly grow into a big costume box. The teacher's corrections are minimal at this point, designed to serve more as a support and encouragement than as a critical standard. The focus is on the delight of dramatic "play," not on a reading exercise which is being judged. Students sense that they are doing this with each other, not for the teacher. With supportive encouragement, students quickly realize that they are able to create widely varying shades of expression. This is appreciated and found entertaining by their classmates--a reward far more appreciated than a grade from the teacher. A hearty round of applause at the conclusion of the enactment caps the "playful" performance.

• Comprehension Check

The next step is a comprehension check which serves to consolidate students' growing understanding. This activity, like the others, is designed to avoid an exercise-like quality. Thus, I begin expressively rephrasing the key lines of the act, pausing to inquire in an interested tone of voice ... "What does that mean in English?" Students answer as a group; they are not called on to answer individually. Occasionally one or two students will begin to dominate the response by answering before everyone else. Rather than asking them to withhold their responses and thereby turning them "off," I quietly acknowledge their contribution with my facial expression and continue asking, both verbally and with my eyes for the answer again--from a different part of the room. The message is subtle, yet effective. The quick responders begin pacing their responses with the rest of the group. The slower responders see that they will be waited for and are valued, and the class does not develop that common split between those who contribute and those who don't.

I avoid allowing this activity to become tedious by keeping my own curiosity and interest level high and by timing the activity according to the engagement level of the group. I end it by asking the group if they understood most of the text already and by generously acknowledging their achievement.

Secondary Activation Activities

In the early stages (0-20 hours) the teacher is the major source of "comprehensible input," through considerable elaborative talking, in order to allow the students to experience their ability to comprehend. Production is not demanded, only invited so as to maintain a low anxiety level. Although students do read material aloud in the primary activation phase, the emphasis is on comprehension as well as production. The ACT Approach shares the premise of Asher, Krashen, Terrell, and others that COMPREHENSION PRECEDES PRODUCTION.

As student comprehension grows and confidence naturally builds, the desire to speak comes automatically. Meeting the natural desire to speak with real opportunities for communication, rather than word drills, is the goal of the secondary activations. This phase is characterized by playful, imaginative, spontaneous ways of encouraging full and authentic receptive and expressive communication.

The Primary Activation Phase is, as the name implies, the first activation of the newly introduced textual material. These activities, as described in the preceding section, stay quite close to a line by line engagement with the text. The Secondary Activation Phase does not attempt to stay so close to the text. The activities of this phase, described below, are much freer variations on the text, picking out idiomatic, syntactical, grammatical constructions and lexical groups for imaginative, playful elaboration. The student may not be consciously aware of the structural focus. His/her attention is directed to the communicative opportunity and example.

Among the types of strategies and activities I have found most effective for the Secondary Activation Phase are:

• Appeal to the Imagination

One of the most powerful ways to tap into the resources of the imagination is to involve students in their own fantasy identity change outlined in Chapter 7. This simple device can be very powerful, encouraging abandonment to a less defensive, more playful and relaxed atmosphere and group interaction. Simply greeting a student with his fantasy name at the beginning of class usually serves to activate the "anchored" positive associations with the identity change and the class. Continuing to chat with him as if the fiction were real will most often spark an outpouring of un-selfconscious imaginative sharing. I may ask what "Heinrich" was up to last night, spotlighting in a gentle way the opportunities for humorous amplification. I usually attempt to link his "story" with the imaginary stories of others in the class, so that quickly and easily a web of light, personal interaction is generated. It is an easy and highly effective way to set a positive, upbeat and productive tone at the start of class.

Other activities appealing to the imagination, such as guided fantasies in the target language, can be very effective tools for elaboration and confidence building. For instance, I often begin a class with a relaxation fantasy bridging this to an imaginative guided journey through a situation containing some content and vocabulary elements from the previous class, thus providing a deep level review. Also, embedding positive suggestions and images relating to the student's self-concept can be helpful. For example, an effective guided fantasy is one suggesting that the student see him/herself interacting in the target language with full confidence and ease, perhaps speaking to one of the engaging characters in the text.

• **Using Props:**

Props of all kinds tie into and enhance all the activities mentioned below:

> * Costume articles, especially hats: these can instantly transform teacher or student into a playful role; jackets, scarves, uniforms, jewelry, etc., all help support an atmosphere of playful communication.

> * Many kinds of physical objects: these can be touched, held, smelled, tasted, moved, passed around, etc., and are extremely useful, especially during the early stages when more Total Physical Response activities are used.

> * Pictures, slides, video tapes: these provide the stimulus for great quantities of comprehensible input and spoken exchange. Terrell and others using the Natural Approach have developed excellent techniques for using pictures.[125] Basic equipment for the Natural Approach teacher is his/her "picture file," (mostly from easily accessible, current magazines)--hundreds of images from many angles of reality, used to enrich context and stimulate reaction.

> * Puppets: See section under this heading at beginning of this chapter.

• **Singing, Miming, and Dancing**

Musical sound, kinesthetic movement and speech can mutually reinforce each other and deepen experientially the learning process. When students see that **singing, gesturing, and dancing can be safe and fun,** they embrace it with gusto. The needed sense of security is more easily available in the fantasy identities and safe atmostphere of the class. Calling upon "Udo" rather than "Jim" to lead the group in a rousing chorus of a song seldom is seen as a threatening challenge, but a playful, and safe chance to try something new and potentially fun.

I find that students love to sing **folksongs**, and a song can be the perfect energy lifter. I like to end before a break on a very positive, upbeat note, so that students leave their seats filled with positive associations to the class. A song serves this purpose well.

Due to my own shyness and lack of experience, **Folk dancing** is something I have tried only rather recently. Once again, I wish I hadn't waited so long. Students love it. Folk dances are wonderful activities for bonding the group and building trust. It is a safe and fun way to make physical contact, laugh, make mistakes, and feel vulnerable collectively-- and, to raise group energy dramatically! Some might worry that the teacher is wasting teaching time on such "non-verbal" activities. Remember, however, that students will be interacting spontaneously in German, and that dancing allows Germanic cultural flavors to penetrate the student at a very basic, physical level.

• Dramatizations

Dramatizing language material in interesting and humorous situations and skits, is basic to the ACT Approach. Students move naturally out of the early phases which focus on listening comprehension into speech production. Playful, dramatic contexts are very helpful in this transition, because they provide the student with a safe, attractive opportunity to use extensive non-verbal contextual cues to promote the communication process. Even in the first weeks, complex communicative interactions are possible without requiring substantial expressive speech. The more communication success a student experiences, the greater the chance of risk-taking the next time.

Short skits, such as finding a seat on a bus, checking in at a hotel, ordering a meal, going through customs, are activities used by many language learning approaches. In the ACT Approach it is not the activity per se, but the special, positive atmosphere in which activities occur, which brings them to life and maintains interest and flow. Once students have truly assented to participate in a positively contagious environment, almost any activity can succeed. Where everyone is wanting and expecting success, there will be success.

• Games

In an atmosphere of play, the conscious focus is not upon students' intentional, linguistic performance, thus allowing them to begin using vocabulary and language structures almost without realizing it. A simple example of how a game can be used is "playing ball," a favorite Lozanov technique. The teacher tosses a large, easy-to-catch ball to a student as s/he asks, for example, "How are you, today?" The student answers while tossing back the ball. The immediate, conscious focus is on catching and throwing the ball, and any strained, expectant attention placed on language production is offset. If the student is hesitant and having verbal difficulty, the ball throwing goes on steadily, while the teacher rephrases the question in such a way as to facilitate success, perhaps offering several choices, such as "great," "so/so," "fantastic."

Card games can be great fun, since much comprehensible input can be generated by all during the interplay. "Strip-21" (a variation on "Blackjack") is a favorite example: Students "bet" with a piece of clothing (a shoe, earring, sweater, etc.--or borrow one, if they are already down to basics), naming the object they bet with as they place it in the center. As cards are turned up, they are named, and the number combinations are counted. The play is usually accompanied by related talk; the spirit is fun, and the language is usually rich and varied.

Again, the effectiveness of these and other games derives less from the specific nature of the activity than from the skillfully created and guided atmosphere in which they occur.

Although the bulk of new vocabulary is presented in the concert sessions, the activation phases continue to offer new input, both in the form of supplementary elaboration and usage skills. Through authentic communication experiences students learn intonation, cadence, timing, and body language. This new input, when authentic, is essential to true communicative competence. It is often neglected in traditional approaches, one reason they are often so lifeless.

The Accelerative Snowball Effect

There is an accelerative "snow-ball effect" when students are succeeding and enjoying themselves. The operating expectation becomes that of success. Risk-taking increases, for it does not lead to "failure" but only to helpful, supportive feedback toward more success. In a climate of mutual support, mistakes may elicit laughter, but it is a "laughing with," not a "laughing at."

The behavioral model of the instructor is crucial in establishing such positive dynamics. His/her authoritative presence lends support to positive dynamics and ignores negative dynamics, allowing negativity to wither for lack of attention. An adage I have found useful:

Whatever we attend to with care — be it opportunities or problems — will grow proportionately.

In sum, the purpose of the activation phases is to assist students to bring to life the material they have received and encoded during the receptive, musical presentations. This is most effectively accomplished without drilling, through activities which playfully stimulate the imagination. A prerequisite for success is a safe and supportive atmosphere which encourages spontaneity and risk-taking.

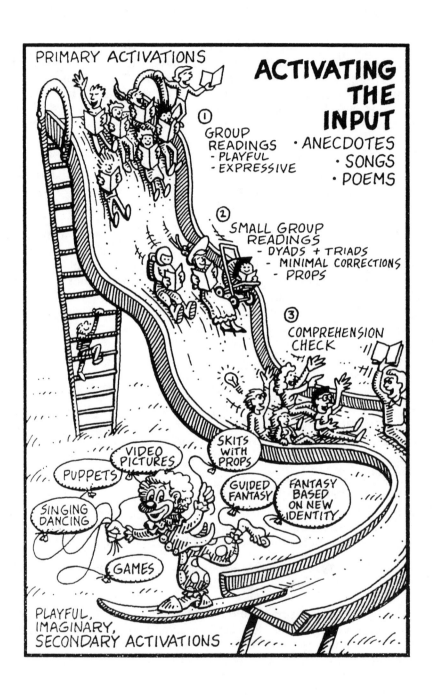

CHAPTER 11

ERROR CORRECTION, GRAMMAR AND HOMEWORK

Error Correction

The ACT Approach, like other acquisition-focused approaches, minimizes direct correction of student errors in speaking. Just as parents do not insist on error-free production as children begin to speak, but rather show delight and affirmation as language communication begins to emerge--so the ACT teacher positively supports and encourages all student speaking attempts. When mistakes occur I may sometimes respond softly, using a positive but correct "echo" of what the student attempted, so that the student is left with both an affirmation <u>and</u> a correct model quietly ringing in her/his ears. The purpose is not so much error correction as providing a confidence check and affirmation. The teacher may expand or slightly and "correctly" rephrase student output in a way to demonstrate to students that meaningful and interesting communication is taking place. Thus, <u>teacher "intervention" serves the flow of conversation.</u>

The objection one most often hears is that without prompt and regular correction students will learn and continually practice incorrect forms, and errors will soon "ossify" into fixed patterns. Indeed, error "ossification" is a phenomenon one can witness in many individuals attempting to speak a foreign language. A very common example is that of the American soldier returning from an assignment in Germany who has learned some primitive "street German" and speaks it with deceptive "fluency". That is, the "German" flows, but its quality is sub-standard, and the soldier may have little or no success in ridding himself of such patterns even if he tries.

I believe, however, that a well-orchestrated language acquisition environment avoids many of the factors which most often produce error ossification. In my view, most native speaking environments are very anxiety producing for beginners in a language. The learner may experience the environment as "threatening" in Hart's sense, and do a brain "downshift" into more primitive survival strategies.[126] The pressure in a native speaking environment is frequently serious: survival tasks must be negotiated. Survival comes first, sophistication later. Sophistication, however, is a quality which comes in an atmosphere where there is room for play and experimentation. One must feel relaxed in order to engage in experimentation. Native speaking environments do not often offer such relaxed settings. Thus, I would argue, it is much more likely for the American soldier, under pressure to accomplish linguistically basic survival tasks to cling to "successful" linguistic patterns, however primitive than the student in a sensitively orchestrated and guided ACT Approach classroom.

All students naturally wish to speak correctly, I believe. If, however, students are placed in a situation where they are forced to speak, and feel that they must come up with enough language to "survive," they may grasp any form that seems to work, however primitive, and hang onto it.

By contrast, in my own experience, when students are invited to speak in a playful context where ego-investment is minimal, students demonstrate new freedom to experiment, and find it easier to abandon what worked yesterday for something more complex and interesting the next day. When the fear level is low there is less clutching to primitive, error-ridden communicative strategies. A natural urge to try something new emerges, just as a small child will experiment with many possible ways to manipulate a toy.

Just as occurs unconsciously in normal child language acquisition, the "pattern-maker" within the brain draws inferences and learns language rules gradually and naturally. The key is relaxed and receptive students in touch with abundant, redundant, yet authentic and "correct" language with little time or attention given to mistakes, especially during the first weeks of a course.

The Role of Grammar

Having as its goal *acquisition*, the ACT Approach gives far less formal attention than language *learning* approaches to the conscious teaching of grammatical concepts. Many teachers want students to learn and apply grammatical rules at the same pace as they learn vocabulary. If language acquisition and authentic communication is the goal, such an equation, as was argued in Chapter 3, will not work. My own experience bears out Krashen's assertion that the conscious study of grammar has only modest value in the acquisition process.[127]

Without taking a radical, "anti-grammar" position, the ACT Approach seeks communicative competence through a balance between "learning" and "acquisition" strategies. The ACT Approach is in fundamental agreement with the following position of Krashen and Terrell in the Natural Approach:

> ... we clearly do want and expect that students will acquire grammar--we do not expect that Natural Approach students will continue to use only simple "stringing" techniques to produce speech. It is also our goal to produce efficient "Monitor users," i.e., those who can Monitor when appropriate without interfering with the flow of communication. Thus, we want to plan for both acquisition opportunities and for learning possibilities where appropriate.

> In embracing a "communication" philosophy, we are not rejecting the idea that students need to acquire (and in some cases learn) a great deal of grammar. In fact, . . . our experience is that they will acquire more grammar this way. Stated simply, focusing on communication goals provides far more comprehensible, meaningful input and encourages more language acquisition, than basing the course on grammar. If we provide discussion, hence input, over a wide variety of topics while pursuing communicative goals, the necessary grammatical structures are automatically provided in the input.[128]

During the ACT class, grammar is presented passively, in the form of attractive, colorful posters displaying structures and paradigms. Posters are affixed to the walls in key locations of the classroom. For example, in displaying past tense forms, a poster will be put up several days before any emphasis of the form is consciously made in class. The purpose of this unique presentation is to allow the students to register abstracted grammar peripherally and semi-consciously. Lozanov offers striking documentation for the effectiveness of this technique.[129] Thus, the powerful semi-conscious level can be activated for the teaching of grammatical material, a task which is traditionally conducted almost exclusively at the conscious, memorization level.

In addition, students are assigned a moderate amount of grammar study and practice exercises at home using the auxiliary text used in the course, without a demand for active mastery. They are thus given deliberate exposure to a comprehensive range of grammatical forms and structures. It is assigned, interesting information, offered as an aid in developing their listening comprehension, reading and writing skills, but de-emphasized in the communicative classroom activities.

Homework

The role of homework is an emotionally charged issue for many teachers as well as students. As teachers we are aware of how much there is to master when studying a second language, and we easily despair at the thought of doing it all in class. It would only seem to make sense that students should perform a great part of the work at home or in the language laboratory. As reasonable as this sounds, homework can, in fact, play more of a negative role than a positive one in the acquisition process. The reason for this is a simple one.

Most homework environments, both physical and psychological, are not compatible with an approach which focuses on acquisition. For most students, homework is associated with exercises and drill. The same is true of most language lab experiences. Thus, an approach such as ACT, which goes to great lengths to establish an optimal climate for acquisition, is very careful in suggesting and structuring work outside class. The skillful teacher, using the appropriate suggestive means and the rich resources of group dynamics, fosters an excellent environment for acquisition within the classroom setting. Outside that environment, however, especially in the early stages, the climate may be very unfavorable. For many students their home study environment is an impoverished one and can be counter-productive. Great care must be exercised to ensure that the positive student attitudes being so carefully nurtured in the classroom are not undermined through needless mechanical and boring work at home.

Traditionally, homework tends to make the student focus on conscious activities about the language. The immense complexity of a language, however, when we try to master it consciously, easily becomes discouraging, as most of us know from our own FL experiences. Conscious acquisition is virtually impossible, because language rules must operate at an unconscious level in natural ways. The early stages of the ACT Approach focus on developing a broad and deep base of comprehension out of which production can naturally emerge. Thus, quantities of written homework are inappropriate, since it is more likely to de-motivate and confuse the student than to help, as it requires a substantially more complex level of competence than can be expected naturally.

There are, however, useful activities which students can, engage in outside of class, which will support the acquisition goals. A primary activity is listening. Most students own or have access to portable audio-cassette players, often with headphones. If they do not, then the language laboratory can be used. Listening activities using one's own personal cassette player are, in my experience, generally welcomed by students. And if the taped materials provide engaging, comprehensible input, motivation will remain high, and the acquisition process will be genuinely furthered. For instance, I provide my students with tapes of the second musical concert readings of the basic ACT text we use. In addition, other texts and variations on them I also tape, giving attention to authenticity of intonation and expression.

Some writing activities, in moderation, can also be useful. I sometimes ask students to transcribe <u>short</u> sentences or paragraphs from tape listening. This activity furthers a visual connection to auditory comprehension, and for some can serve to sharpen their auditory acuity. Some types of Cloze exercises are good; for example, students are given a written text with key words missing, needing to be filled in. In the early stages it is important that the missing words not require grammatical manipulation, thus most nouns are appropriate. This activity stimulates the student's sense of contextual understanding, rather than asking for a conscious capacity to manipulate grammatical forms. The latter may become a positive reinforcer somewhat later.

One outside activity I regularly suggest to students is to read over the dramatic and/or dialog texts lightly--as one would an interesting magazine article--just before going to sleep--accompanied by the second ("passive") concert presentation of the same material recorded on cassette and furnished for their personal use. From a theoretical point of view, as the day's conscious hold begins relaxing its control, an anchoring effect can occur in the more receptive mind.

Conscious learning tasks do, however, become increasingly appropriate later in the course as the skills of reading and writing receive greater attention. Conscious skill-learning is then useful given there is time to offer and apply such skills. Somewhere after 25-30 hours of focusing on listening and oral skills, student motivation and interest is usually high enough to sustain some conscious attention on language mechanics, grammar and syntax. In Level 2 of the ACT program, especially, I focus increasingly on conscious, learned mastery, especially in the areas of reading and writing. Here, also, I give care to avoid suggesting a traditional "learning" orientation.

Although the ACT approach relies relatively less than other methods on student efforts outside class, some students will want home-work. Many students derive desired security from being able to expend large amounts of effort alone to master assigned tasks. I explain to students that they will have optimum success as they learn to tap their vast uncon-scious resources and relax their conscious controls. This can be a threatening prospect for certain students, who need encouragement and affirming sup-port in order to trust capacities they are unaware are present. Their rapid gains in acquisition skills during the first weeks usually present enough concrete evidence to overcome initial doubts.

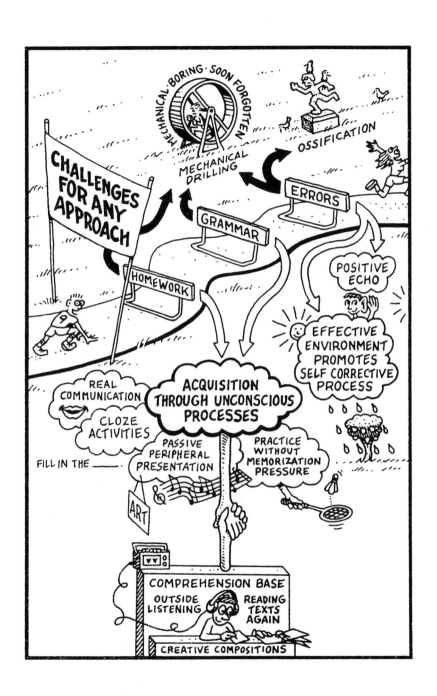

CHAPTER 12

DOCUMENTED RESULTS I
The ACT Courses at the University of Massachusetts at Boston

Although carefully controlled and measured programs in language acquisition approaches are few, their numbers are growing. The results of such studies are adding stronger and stronger support for a shift away from language "learning" to language "acquisition."[130] Among the first American academic applications of the theory of suggestion to an acquisition approach have been the German courses which I offered at the University of Massachusetts at Boston, 1979-90, in which the constantly evolving ACT Approach has been used. A description of those courses and their results is the subject of this chapter. The next chapter is a report on the Fort Devens experiment using ACT, where more formal, controlled and thorough evaluation was possible.

ACT German Courses at the University of Massachusetts at Boston

After completing training in Suggestopedia from Dr. Georgi Lozanov in 1979, I returned to the University of Massachusetts at Boston and implemented a suggestopedic German course as faithful to Lozanov's model as I was able to create. Over the years since that first course in 1979,

I have developed the ACT Approach, which has Lozanov's Suggestopedia as its foundation, but it has been gradually transformed and enriched by the work of Krashen, Terrell, Asher, Hart (all of whom have been discussed at length in earlier chapters) and by many others. Since that first course in 1979 I have offered nine 90-hour Level I and eight 90-hour Level II German courses at the University of Massachusetts at Boston, using the ACT Approach which was going though a steady evolution during these years. The results have been exciting and highly encouraging. Although the courses have not been conducted within a formal design for controlled evaluation, much evaluative evidence has been gathered. The following sections describe in detail how the classes were set up and conducted as well as report the results of a variety of means of evaluation.

Two types of ACT Courses have been developed:

- **Level 1,** roughly equivalent to two semesters of regular college German.

- **Level 2,** roughly the "equivalent" to two semesters of regular college Intermediate German.

Both Level I and Level 2 ACT are offered in the same, single semester, carrying a total of 16 semester credits in one semester.

ACT German: Level I

- **Students**

  ‣ There are only two criteria for selecting students:
    - No previous study of German.
    - Maximum 20 hours per week of outside work at a job.

  ‣ Class size varies from 12 to 16, with a balance between males and females.

  ‣ Ages range from 20-54 years old, with the average in the mid-twenties.

- **Class Format**

    The class meets for three 60-minute periods (9-12:30 with breaks), five days per week for six weeks (90 hours total).

• Method

The method for the course is the ACT Approach as described in the earlier chapters of this book.

• Physical Setting

The courses are conducted in a room decorated and furnished for suggestive purposes:

- Rug on the floor
- Relaxing, comfortable chairs with arms and head rest
- Softened, adjustable lighting or full-spectrum fluorescent lighting
- Stereo-cassette music system
- Video-taping available
- Colorful wall posters and charts and maps
- Easels with flip charts and/or white boards with colorful markers
- Plants and/or fresh cut flowers
- Refreshment area with hot water for chocolate, tea, coffee, etc.

• Instructional Materials

- A basic suggestopedic text: *Eine deutsche Reise,* originally written by Charles Schmid and substantially rewritten by myself.
- A supplementary text as a reference for grammar, structure, and supplementary readings[131]
- Songs
- Short reading passages
- Overhead transparencies (with song texts, pictures of objects for TPR activities, cartoons, etc.)
- Many props (puppets, costume articles, objects, clocks, maps, cards, etc.)
- Extensive collection of colorful pictures on wide-ranging topics

• Credits

The Level 1 course (titled German 110: Experiencing German I) carries double semester credit (8) for the six-week sequence.

• Grades

Students for Level 1 are not graded in a traditional manner. For most of the courses they have had one of two options:

▸ Pass / Fail, where regular attendance guarantees a Pass
▸ The same grade as their cumulative grade point average upon entering the course.
  Suggestive theory postulates that fear is the single greatest obstacle to learning. The rationale for a non-graded course was that testing and grading engender--in the form of fear of failure--the greatest anxiety factors for most students. During the first hour of the course the issue of grades is put out of the way. The purpose of this strategy is to enable students to abandon themselves more freely and fully to a safe, supportive and stimulating environment. Thus, they might experience and discover German and themselves through the human adventure of communication.

• Requirements

The only requirement for most of the courses has been regular attendance. Students are told they will be asked to withdraw or receive an F after five unexcused absences. No such circumstance has arisen. During the first course, one student missed one class. The other eleven students had perfect attendance records. In the second course, two students missed one class apiece. In the third, one student dropped the course and withdrew from the university after three absences (for personal reasons); two other students missed one class apiece. During the fourth course, two students missed two classes and two missed one class. This has been the typical pattern.

These attendance records are unmatched in my previous 14 years of teaching. I believe that the explanation goes beyond any "attendance requirement." One student wrote on the post-course evaluation form: "I've enjoyed every single minute of class ..." Another wrote: "I looked forward to going to school every day because of this class."

• Evaluation and Testing

At the end of many of these courses standardized tests have been administered. But clearly, the most meaningful evaluation of the effectiveness and the success of the course has been established in other ways. First, there have been video-taped records. The entire first two Level 1 courses (180 hours total) were recorded on video tape with two cameras and split screen mixing, allowing more than one dimension of the communicative process to be seen simultaneously. Second, there have been numerous observational visits from colleagues, who could observe through a one-way window without influencing the environment. Also, there have been oral and written evaluations done by the instructor and the students. At the conclusion of the most recent four courses, I have administered the Oral Proficiency Interview, [after receiving OPI training by ACTFL (The American Council on the Teaching of Foreign Languages)].

▶ Videotaping and Outside Observers

The video tapes provide testimony capturing the immediacy of a delightful and effective learning experience. Various sequences have been shown to several thousand FL teachers throughout the U.S., and the response has been overwhelmingly favorable: teachers desire in their own classes the kind of enthusiastic, motivated and authentic communication which is displayed on the tapes.

Observational visits by professional colleagues produced an overwhelmingly favorable response to the students' motivation, enthusiasm, spontaneity and desire to communicate in German. Some colleagues have been concerned about grammatical imprecision and its potential implication for upper-level course work. There has also been concern that the approach might require a level of instructor engagement and spontaneity which is uncommon among university FL teachers.

Initially I was unsure about how to respond to the criticism that the students' grammar was flawed. During the first four courses I was unacquainted with Krashen's work and his distinction between "learning" and "acquisition." I sensed, however, that for the first time in my classes "real" language was being understood and spoken, and that students were delighted with the process of acquiring and using another language. I saw that their grammar was imprecise, although naturally and unconsciously applied. I realized that they would not be able to perform well on the discrete point grammar tests used in regular classes. Rather than back away from this criticism, I decided to follow the positive flow of student responses being generated in my new classes, and to work on refinements later. I am glad about my decision, for I now understand that an early insistence on precision will most probably have a dulling, if not de-accelerating effect on FL acquisition.

After only three weeks of the course some colleagues came to me and asked what could be making the students so willing to speak German to them and other students outside of class. They found my students more willing to speak German to them than most graduating senior majors.

▶ The Students' Own Post-Course Evaluations

The students themselves gave eloquent testimony to their learning satisfaction. The majority of students (80% of whom were juniors and seniors) wrote that "Experiencing German" had been the most enjoyable and valuable course they had ever had. This hardly represented a typical reaction to a beginning foreign language course! Three representative student course evaluations:

Student 1:
> *This class is magic! It brought out the best in me to facilitate learning--my child naturally, which laughs and plays and learns with open doors; my adult which appreciates the spirit of music, poetry and personal interaction as well as intellectual satisfaction of learning a new language. The primary element which made this possible was Lynn. He himself embodies the creative spontaneity of a child and the philosophical and spiritual awareness one gains through experience. As a student I felt his genuineness--he tapped my trust and set me free to learn without anxiety. The material was well-organized. I appreciate the integration of music, poetry, and culture with the fundamentals of the German language.*
> *I could go on and on--that in itself reflects the impact of the course on me. I'll take not only the language with me, but also the experience.*

Student 2:
> *Easily, this class wins out as the best I've ever taken! I've found Lynn to be a wonderfully supportive and patient instructor-- perfect for this joyful learning experience. I've enjoyed every single minute of class: every game, story, explanation, etc. was packed with vocabulary, grammar, lessons, cultural anecdotes which I found very valuable. I'm amazed at my ability to speak German in class. I've taken language courses before and never found the experiences with them as exhilarating, as thorough, as therapeutic as this one. An added plus for this course is that I've been able to carry the same level of energy I've had in this class into my other courses, and this course makes learning*

much less stressful. If I've learned nothing else (certainly not true) I've learned especially that I can.

Student 3:

I am a senior, who has taken a wide variety of courses, all successfully, and this course has been by far the best I have had. Although I know that much of its success can be attributed to the instructor, his versatility and nurturing manner, it is also the method itself--learning something with one's whole being is an experience I've not had since I was a child. Our school systems do not cater to this kind of learning. Even though this course requires intense amounts of energy and concentration, it gives rather than drains, and at the end of each day I am invigorated. We have become a family here, and I will be sorry to say "Auf Wiedersehen" to these people with whom I've learned so much. I strongly believe that all learning can be structured in similar ways to become more valuable. We all have experienced more than just words of a specific language: we have experienced a culture, understood a new people, a new land and felt something of what it must be like to be German. After 90 hours of this method I speak better German than I spoke French after 4 years as a straight A French student.
I have nothing but glowing praise for everything about this course.

▶ Testing

Some measure of how a program performs in helping students attain desired outcomes is essential. There is often pressure from administrators for documentation which will allow comparisons with other programs or courses. This pressure is understandable but problematical, since different programs or courses often have different objectives, teach different content, and consequently, should test differently. There appears to be little value in comparing the test scores of one group of students whose "linguistic" competence is being measured with another group whose "communicative" competence is being evaluated.

In the ACT courses described above, where students wished to advance to intermediate or advanced levels--levels which presupposed language "learning" rather than "acquisition", it was important to ascertain how the "acquisition" group compared with traditional FL standards. At the end of the course I administered the standardized MLA exam in German. This exam is designed for students who have completed two semesters of college study. So as to have some basis for comparison with the regular departmental program, one of my colleagues agreed to administer the same test to her second semester elementary course. The exam tests listening comprehension and speaking (in quite unauthentic contexts, to be sure), reading comprehension, discrete point grammatical knowledge, and writing skills.

Two successive ACT Level 1 classes (a total of 25 students) were given the MLA tests. The results were better than expected. My student's scores ranged from the 55th to the 75th percentile, whereas my colleague's students scored between the 60th and 80th percentiles, only slightly higher scores despite the fact that they had studied many hours at home for two semesters in their attempts to master grammar. The ACT students scored excellently, in spite of the artificial contexts, on listening comprehension and speaking. Their ease and flexibility with their basic knowledge probably accounts for the fact that they also did rather well on the reading comprehension sections. Their lowest performances understandably came on the discrete point grammar section and in the writing section.

The MLA test is an inappropriate instrument to measure the effectiveness of ACT courses, since it measures "learning", not "acquisition". I chose to use it, knowing that the ACT students would be at a great disadvantage, but curious to see how well they could perform for "learning" standards. I was gratified with the results, but I stopped administering that test, since it appears somewhat punishing and not conducive to suggestive goals to submit students to a test for which the course does not prepare them.

▶ The Oral Proficiency Interview (OPI)

My search for an appropriate means to evaluate and validate the impressive accomplishments of the ACT students resulted in the discovery of the Oral Proficiency Interview (OPI), originally developed by the U. S. Foreign Service Institute and then adapted for regular school students by the American Council for the Teaching of Foreign Languages (ACTFL). ACTFL states:

> The oral interview is a test of an individual's foreign language speaking ability. The interview is a seemingly casual, but highly

structured, face-to-face conversation with a trained tester for a period generally ranging from 10-20 minutes. The resulting speech sample is then rated on a scale ranging from no practical ability to ability equivalent to that of an educated native. The ratings assigned by the tester represent ranges of proficiency rather than points on a scale.[132]

The ACTFL-OPI ratings range from levels of Novice, Intermediate, Advanced to Superior. Each of these levels is further broken down into sub-levels. The ACTFL "Generic" Proficiency Guidelines characterize the main divisions as follows:

The Novice level is characterized by the ability to communicate minimally with learned material.

The Intermediate level is characterized by the ability to:
-- *create with the language by combining and recombining learned elements, through primarily in a reactive mode;*
-- *initiate, minimally sustain, and close in a simple way basic communicative tasks; and*
-- *ask and answer questions.*

The Advanced level is characterized by the speaker's ability to:
-- *converse in a clearly participatory fashion;*
-- *initiate, sustain, and bring to closure a wide variety of communicative tasks, including those that require an increased ability to convey meaning with diverse language strategies due to a complication or an unforeseen turn of events;*
-- *narrate and describe with paragraph-length connected discourse.*

The Superior level is characterized by the speaker's ability to:
-- *participate effectively in most formal and informal conversations on practical, social, professional, and abstract topics; and*
-- *support opinions and hypothesize using native-like discourse strategies.*[133]

A full description of the ACTFL guidelines for speaking proficiency in German is duplicated in Appendix 3.

In 1985 I participated in the ACTFL training in OPI for FL teachers at Georgetown University. Since that time I have used the Oral Proficiency Interview to evaluate ACT students after the six week Level I course, and then again after twelve weeks, upon completion of Level II. Ideally, for the OPI results to be as unbiased as possible, a trained interviewer different from the class instructor, unfamiliar with the students, should conduct the interviews. This is, however, logistically and financially difficult. For the Fort Devens project, described in the next chapter, where a formal evaluation structure was used, a trained OPI interviewer was contracted to evaluate the student interviews. For my regular university courses, I conduct the interviews myself and keep the video recordings as objective evidence.

At present the OPI is the best tool I know to evaluate a students ability to speak a foreign language in a closely approximated authentic communication context. Without going into the theoretical considerations and detailed structure of the OPI, since extensive discussion and material on the interview is readily available from ACTFL,[134] the following description will give the reader unfamiliar with the OPI an idea of what it entails.

Upon conclusion of the course, I make individual appointments of 15 minutes each with all students. They are told that the purpose of the interview is to collect data for research purposes. The interview does not affect their grade or credit for the course. With nothing at stake, students are able to be more themselves and relax into a more authentic conversation.

For the OPI I arrange the room comfortably with two comfortable chairs facing each other a little obliquely to avoid a more confrontive head-to-head arrangement. I record all the interviews so as to have a permanent record. I personally find it easier and a better record to videotape the interviews. The camera with built-in mike is placed 8-10 feet away, and is less obtrusive than a tape recorder with its mikes placed more closely.

The interview is conducted entirely in the target language. I begin with a somewhat artificial introduction ("Hello, my name is Lynn Dhority.") as a cue for the student to identify him or herself for the taped record. After that the interview proceeds as what may appear to be a rather informal conversation, with the interviewer curiously gathering information about the student's life, thoughts and opinions. As casual as the "conversation" may appear, it has a specific structure, moving from topics requiring basic, concrete vocabulary and structures to more complex topics involving the different tenses and moods. The student is usually asked to role-play a situation with the interviewer, which involves various degrees of problem solving and asking questions on the part of the student. As soon as it is apparent where the student's highest level of sustained competence lies, the interviewer probes beyond that level to determine with certainty that the student cannot sustain a higher level and observes where "linguistic breakdown" occurs. Then he drops back to the highest level which the student can sustain. That level is the basis for the rating.[135] The interviewer always guides the student to a level of comfortable competence before ending the interview, so as to end on a successful note. A friendly conclusion and the interview is over, lasting from 10 to 15 minutes.

The majority of ACT Level 1 students achieve after the intensive six-week course an ACTFL Speaking Proficiency Level of Intermediate-Mid. The ACTFL Guidelines describe Intermediate-Mid proficiency in German speaking as:

Intermediate--Mid

Able to satisfy most routine travel and survival needs and some limited social demands. Can ask and answer questions on very familiar topics and in areas of immediate need. Can initiate and respond to simple statements, and can maintain simple face-to-face conversation. Can ask and answer questions and carry on a conversation on topics beyond basic survival needs or involving the exchange of personal information, i.e., can talk simply about autobiographical information, leisure time activities, academic subjects. Can handle simple transactions at the post office, bank, drugstore, etc. Misunderstandings arise because of limited vocabulary, frequent grammatical errors, and poor pronunciation and intonation, although speakers at this level have broader vocabulary and/or greater grammatical and phonological control than speakers at Intermediate-Low. Speech is often characterized by long pauses. Some grammatical accuracy in some basic structures, i.e., subject-verb agreement, word order in simple statements (excluding adverbs) and interrogative forms, present tense of irregular verbs and imperative of separable prefix verbs *(Kommen Sie mit!)*. Fluency is still strained but may be quite natural while within familiar territory. Is generally understood by persons used to dealing with foreigners.

Occasionally a student will be at Intermediate Low and occasionally one may achieve Intermediate High. See Appendix 3 for a description of these ratings.

• Conclusions

Since careful research design or controls for these ACT Level 1 classes were not possible, no objectively verifiable conclusions can be drawn. The experience and available evidence has been, however, very encouraging. All students enrolled in the ACT course experienced positive, satisfying study of a foreign language. Unlike other FL courses offered at my university, which experience an attrition rate in the elementary courses of 25-50%, there was minimal attrition in the ACT courses. In addition, no students left the ACT course experiencing failure in FL study. And, unlike other beginning FL courses, where less than 50% of the students continue on to more advanced levels, 90% of the ACT students elected to continue German on to Level 2.

The ACT students' strong motivation for further study presented a challenge for me as the instructor. The existing departmental Intermediate offerings did not seem appropriate for students completing the ACT course. My students were coming from an intensive immersion in listening, speaking, and communicating, both expressively and spontaneously. A conventional Intermediate course, with grammar review exercises and read-and-answer-the-questions, seemed like a cold shower shock. I postulated that what was needed was a second course, designed to capitalize on the confidence and motivation of my students, one which could provide an engaging transition to the level of precision needed for advanced study and/or independent work in the new language. Thus, I developed and offered a Level 2 course, again using the ACT Approach. ACT Level II is the subject of the next section.

ACT German: Level II

• Rationale

Alfred North Whitehead has said that an educational process needs to begin with a "romance" phase. Here the student experiences the exhilaration of new vistas and horizons and the potential power of knowledge which lies waiting to be claimed. Only after the romance experience, said Whitehead, should the student embark upon the next phase, that of "precision." One needs, he implied, the ardor of the lover to withstand the challenges on the pathway to mastery. My own experience in learning and teaching has taught me to embrace Whitehead's thought.

The experience of Level 1 students had been one of <u>success</u>. Their evaluations indicated that the learning experience had indeed been a "romance" in Whitehead's sense. All of the students succeeded in completing an intensive learning experience in German. They all knew in a down-to-earth way that they could learn another language, and were, in fact, fully in the process of doing so. Their confidence was as high as their motivation for more learning. They were also aware that their skills were still rudimentary. Their confidence and motivation had led them to reach further for precision and mastery. For me it seemed clear that <u>now</u> was the moment to begin blending more formal "learning" with "acquisition." Now students were ready to begin thinking "about" the language. They now had a good foundation and would be ready to develop what Krashen has termed the "monitor," that is, conscious refinement and application of language rules. Now was the time for Whitehead's "precision" phase.

• **Level 2 Objectives**

  ‣ To maintain the positive atmosphere which had been established in Level 1 and continue the acquisition process to more advanced levels of communicative competence.

  ‣ To add increasingly a conscious "learning" component in the form of grammar study outside of class and writing assignments for conscious practice in developing the "monitor" function.[136]

  ‣ To help students attain both acquired and learned mastery which would enable them to:

    ▼ enter more advanced university language and/or literature courses.
    ▼ study abroad in a German-speaking country.
    ▼ do independent study and research.
    ▼ travel, work, or live successfully in a German-speaking environment.

• **Students**

The students for Level 2 are nearly all drawn from Level 1. The few who do not continue usually stop for financial or other personal reasons. As an experiment, one or two students have been occasionally admitted to Level 2 who had not taken ACT Level 1 but had undergone some other preparation. The entrance of the newcomers into the previously well-established group dynamics involving play and fantasy have been quite challenging for all concerned. For me the challenge has been to facilitate the adjustment in the interest of everyone. In some courses the new students adjust quickly; in others, they never become as fully comfortable as the continuing students. My own skill in facilitating the transition has grown, however, and I feel confident and positive about mixing students.

• Class Format and Physical Environment

The class format is the same as Level 1, meeting 9:00-12:30, five days per week for six weeks for a total of 90 hours. This presents no scheduling problem for most students, since they have already arranged their courses in order to take Level 1 for the first 6 weeks of the semester. Thus, students are able to take both intensive courses in the same semester.

The physical environment is the same as for Level 1.

• Method

Variations on the ACT Approach are used. The underlying principles and assumptions remain the same.

Students retain their fantasy identities and life-roles, although they are given an opportunity to change, if they wish. Newly incoming students choose an new identity. Much new material is introduced through concert sessions, but a considerable amount of reading is assigned outside of class. The class reads short stories and plays by well-known German authors. Much of the assigned material is re-enacted in skits or actual drama performances. A wide range of communication activities fill most of the class time.

I assign nightly activities with the supplementary text (grammar study, brief exercises, short compositions, reading selections). I respond to the assignments daily with encouraging feedback, indicating how much is correct, how conscious understanding is growing, and what types of errors might profitably be addressed for the next day's assignment. Short, ungraded quizzes on grammatical form are given frequently.

Students keep a personal journal in German, and this written work is handed in twice a week for feedback from the instructor.

Thus, reading, writing, and conscious grammar study was added to the ongoing class-time emphasis on communication.

• Materials

I use commercially available materials and supplement them heavily with poems, songs, films, video tapes, music cassettes, etc. Books I typically use:

➻ *Der Weg Zum Lesen,* a collection of short stories, edited by Vail and Sparks
➻ *Der Besuch der alten Dame,* a play by F. Dürrenmatt.
➻ *Biedermann und die Brandstifter,* a play by Max Frisch.
➻ A supplementary language textbook, begun in Level 1 – such as *Alles Gute* by Briggs and Crean.
➻ *Geheime Mission,* a series of spy episodes which I introduce with cassettes before giving students the written version.

In addition I use numerous short xeroxed selections from a wide variety of sources, often introducing them through a Concert Presentation.

• Credits

Eight semester hours of credit are granted for the Level 2 sequence. Thus, in one semester, it is possible for students to take both Levels 1 and 2 and to receive sixteen semester hours of credit in German. This is the same amount of credit earned by students who take four semester of regular German.

• Requirements

All students are required to attend regularly. After two unexcused absences, each further absence automatically lowers their chosen grade option (see below) by 1/2 grade. Students rarely exceed the allowed number of absences.

• Grades

Grades are difficult to reconcile with the ACT Approach. To grade a student places the instructor in the role of judge, yet the ACT teacher is most effective in the role of coach/facilitator. I have experimented with a variety of grading formulas and alternatives and the best solution for Level 2 has been to handle grades in a contractual manner, thus making the instructor's role more one of coach/bookkeeper than judge. Students are offered three options:

▸ For a C, students are required to attend regularly and hand in their German journal punctually.

▸ For a B, students are required, in addition to the requirements for a C, to hand in all reading comprehension and
grammar exercises punctually.

▸ For an A, students, in addition to the requirements for a C
and B, are required to read a selection (approximately
10-15 pages) from either Nietzsche, Hesse, Marx, Schurz,
or Büchner, write an essay in German in answer to assigned questions on the reading, and translate a specified
passage into English.

Approximately 20% of the students chose the C option, 50% the B
option, and 30% the A option.

● Evaluation, Testing, and Results

As can be seen from the above, grades are given for easily quan-
tifiable performances: 1) being present; 2) writing out assignments;
3) reading material and answering comprehension questions. The grade
options are intended to provide meaningful choices, depending on the
motivation and time resources available to the student. These home
assigned "learning" tasks are not "graded", i.e. qualitatively ranked;
rather, they are recorded simply as having been completed. This is
designed to mitigate the role of the teacher as judge, whose "verdict"
(from the student's point of view) might remain an uncertain, continuing
source of anxiety. The ungraded assignments are, however, given lengthy
responses in terms of supportive comments and suggestions for improvement.
This is done to promote the teacher in the role of supportive guide/coach.

"Acquisition" activities are neither quantified nor graded. The
requirement of regular attendance virtually assures continuing acquisition,
depending, of course, upon the skill of the instructor. A teacher can
"require" the completion of conscious learning tasks. One cannot
meaningfully "require" acquisition, which occurs, as it does in children
learning language, largely at a sub-conscious level. One can, however, trust
that in an appropriate environment such as the one designed for these
classes, acquisition will occur automatically. I believe that this
assumption has been born out by the results of these classes.

I attempt to separate evaluation and testing components from the
grading component. The grade options offers students choices concerning the
degree and type of mastery they wished to attain. Grades are not allowed
to serve as a judgment concerning ability, quality, or performance. Some
form of assessment is, however, needed regarding the effectiveness of the

class in helping students reach their own, individual learning objectives and also the objectives of the university and department curriculum.

Feedback on the course is obtained as follows:

- Video tapes of communication activities, skits, and a final, major drama performance provide an accurate and encompassing record of spontaneous and prepared communication activities. These are valuable documentation aids for measuring the students' communicative competence.

- Regular written quizzes covering grammatical information, learned from the supplementary text, provides documentation of the "learning" component.

- Frequent visits from professional colleagues again provides a regular source of additional perspective and comparison.

- The students' post-course evaluations describes the value of the course in relation to their own objectives. (These evaluations have been unanimously positive.)

- What students have done with their knowledge of German after completing the course has also served as documentation of students' capacities:

  - Approximately 10% of the students have been able after the one intensive ACT semester (12 weeks of Level 1 and Level 2) to enter and complete successfully the sixth semester of the regular German curriculum entitled "Advanced Conversation and Composition." Of these students, one went on from there to enter the University of Freiburg, Germany, for a highly successful year. This student returned the following year to complete a major in German. She thereupon received a full scholarship for graduate study in German at a major university.

  - Approximately 80% of the students continue German in a course generally taken in the fourth or fifth semester of the regular curriculum. This course focuses on conversational skills.

  - 30-40% of the students find some means to travel to Germany or Austria during the summer following the course.

⥤ Approximately 20-30% of the students apply for admission to and are accepted in our year-long study program in Baden-Württemberg, Germany.

▸ Standardized Testing

CLEP

At the end of the 12 weeks, depending on the availability of financial support, I periodically administer the standardized CLEP[137] exam designed for students who have completed four semesters of college German. This test is a better instrument than the MLA exam, since unlike the latter it attempts to measure only listening comprehension and reading comprehension. Nevertheless, it is clear that the CLEP, too, is primarily designed for students who have been focusing on "learning" rather than "acquiring" a new language. The results, based on thirty students taking the exam in two different years, can be summarized as follows:

90th percentile or above:	10% of ACT students
80th	35%
70th	35%
60th	15%
56th	3%
lower	none

The Oral Proficiency Interview (OPI)

Just as in the case of ACT Level 1, at the conclusion of Level 2 each student is given the OPI. See the discussion of OPI earlier in this chapter for a description of the interview. The format for the interview for Level 2 students does not change substantially, only the content of the interview is more sophisticated and probes into higher levels of communicative competence.

Whereas Level 1 students experience a rapid leap in increased competence, from Novice Low[138] to Intermediate Mid in most cases, such a quantum leap is not to be expected at the more advanced levels, where time-won mastery are required.

The majority of ACT Level 2 students achieve the Intermediate High level on the OPI. The ACTFL Profiency

Guidelines describe this level of proficiency in German speaking as follows:

Intermediate--High

Able to satisfy most survival needs and limited social demands. Developing flexibility in language production although fluency is still uneven. Can initiate and sustain a general conversation on factual topics beyond basic survival needs. Can give autobiographical information and discuss leisure time activities. Most verbs are still in the present tense, more common past participles appear *(gegangen, gesehen, geschlafen)*. Many mistakes in choice of auxiliary *(habe gegangen* with the present perfect). Past tense is attempted also with common imperfect forms *(sagte, hatte, war)*. Several high-frequency separable prefix verbs appear in the indicative *(ich gehe mit)*. There is inconsistent coding of proper dative and accusative cases following prepositions in singular and plural. Attempts to expand discourse which is only accurate in short sentences. Frequently gropes for words. Comprehensible to native speakers used to dealing with foreigners, but still has to repeat utterances frequently to be understood by the general public.[139]

About 15% of the ACT Level 2 students reach Intermediate Mid, and an occasional student reaches the Advanced Level. I have had three students out of a total of 125 reach Advanced.[140]

‣ Videotaped Drama Performance

One of the most revealing pieces of documentation emerging from Level 2 is the video taped record of a drama performance of several full scenes (approximately one hour) from F. Dürrenmatt's drama, *Der Besuch der alten Dame (The Visit)*. All students participate in a production of this play, which contains challenging characterizations and many characters. Each student plays several different roles of varying difficulty. These tapes have been shown to numerous professional colleagues. The judgment has been uniform: these students have acquired remarkable proficiency at many levels, including authentic intonation, pronunciation, cadence, and body language. Such abilities clearly surpass what could be drilled into students for a fast performance. In short, the students have developed a degree of real fluency in the art of authentic communication. This assertion is further supported by the fact that rehearsals for these performances occupy only a portion of class time.

• Conclusions

The Level 2 ACT German course provides students with an opportunity to continue rapid *acquisition* of the language while at the same time introducing an intensive *learning* component. By the end of the twelve-week course students are prepared to use German in authentic communication contexts at a skill level ranging from the Intermediate Mid to Intermediate High Levels on the ACTFL Oral Proficiency scale. Also, they are able to continue on to more advanced academic levels of study, from the 5th to 6th semester level of normal college study. Thus, a bridge is created between the budding communicative competence emerging in Level 1 and the more traditional demands of foreign language study. Many students consider Level 2 to be an appropriate terminal course for formal, classroom language study, and I would support that judgment. Upon conclusion of Level 2, students are ready to seek "input" from a wide range of sources, many of them superior to a classroom. As Krashen has pointed out: •

> The classroom should help only to the extent it supplies comprehensible input in an environment conducive to a low filter. This may indeed be . . . its main function. . . it should be especially valuable for beginners, those who cannot easily utilize the informal environment for input. It will be of less value to those who can, who have other sources of comprehensible input, and who are linguistically advanced enough to take advantage of it.[141]

These courses using the ACT Approach at the University of Massachusetts at Boston provide the basis for ongoing experimentation and adaptation. These experiments have generated interest in many teachers and administrators throughout the country, and I have conducted seminars and teacher training programs for hundreds of teachers on the ACT Approach.

In the next chapter I report on the experimental ACT program which I conducted at the invitation of the U.S. Army at Fort Devens, Massachusetts, in the spring of 1983. The Fort Devens project offered the opportunity to utilize more controlled evaluation measures, and the results offer strong support for the effectiveness of ACT.

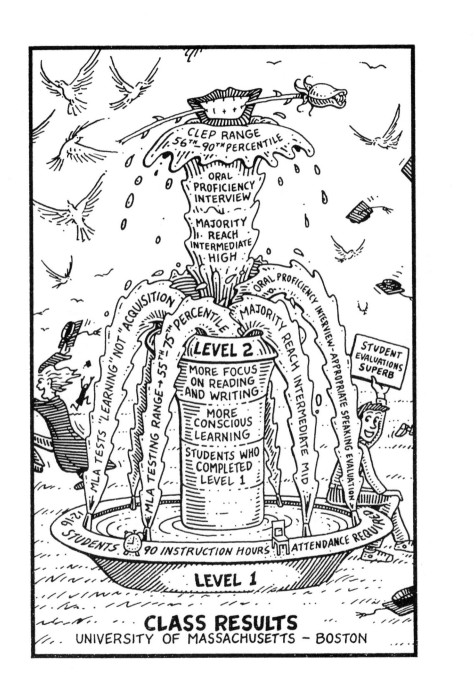

CLASS RESULTS
UNIVERSITY OF MASSACHUSETTS – BOSTON

CHAPTER 13

THE ACT APPROACH FOR THE U.S. ARMY
A Documented Experiment

This chapter provides a descriptive, documented account of a beginning FL language course using the ACT Approach within a more controlled experimental environment than was the setting at the University of Massachusetts. The intent is to describe the actual program and its results with an immediacy that enables the reader to better sense what it can be like to apply ACT principles in a concrete situation.

Background

In the spring, 1982, the director of foreign language programs for the army at Fort Devens, MA, invited me to conduct an experimental pilot program in German for military personnel using the ACT Approach. I was cautious in accepting an invitation to use this very humanistic approach in a military environment. The positive opportunity, however, outweighed my reservations. The controlled nature of the project, involving a challenging population, promised to provide much needed data on the effectiveness of the ACT Approach in non-college settings.

• Purpose

The purpose of the experiment was to compare the ACT Approach with a variation of the standard audio-lingual program designed by the Defense Language Institute in Monterey, California, which was currently being used at Fort Devens.

• Objectives

The teaching objective of the experiment was to enable students to achieve better results and, if possible, to do so in a shorter time period than with the program currently in use. The specific behavioral objective was for the students to score a rating of number 1 or better on the DLI/FSI[142] scale for listening, reading and speaking skills, as measured by standard and oral tests administered following language training.

Prior to the experimental ACT program, the objective of the language program at Fort Devens had been to bring personnel to a skill level of number 1 on the Defense Language Institute (DLI) skillrating scale for listening and reading. (This scale is essentially the same as the Foreign Service Institute/FSI scale.)[143] Speaking, considered an equally important skill, was also tested, although not by any standardized means. In the majority of cases the above objective had not been met following a standard 12-week, 360 hour course. Thus, the search for a more effective program.

Description of Course

• Student Selection

A typical, 12-man military unit was selected--composed of a Captain (the ranking officer), a 1st Lieutenant, a team Sergeant and nine other non-commissioned officers. This represented a sample, a group typical of the groups which would need future instruction as judged by officers in charge of the experimental project.

The group size was enlarged to 13 by the addition of the director of the Fort Devens language programs, who had received no previous instruction in German.

• Language Background

Many armed services personnel have had previous foreign language instruction or foreign language experience through foreign assignments. The experimental team was typical in this respect. All but two team members had undergone a 12-week, 360-hour intensive course in

Czech one year before this experimental program. As summarized in Table 1, all but two students had been exposed to German either in school or abroad before the beginning of the German course.

	Table 1	
	Foreign Language Background	
	Previous Instruction in German	Assignment Time in Germany
M.B.	None	7 years
J.C.	5 years in school	None
R.G.	None	5 years
M.H.	None	12 weeks
J.J.	2 years in high school	None
W.M.	None	None
J.M.	None	4 1/2 months
C.P.	None	4 months
W.R.	None	4 years
D.T.	2 years in college	1 month
V.W.	None	3 years
C.W.	None	None

● Disparity in Linguistic Background

As may be inferred from Table 1, students are grouped by team affiliation, not by virtue of their skill or competence level in the language. Thus, in any given team there may well be students who already possess basic communicative competence as well as students who have never been exposed to any language other than English. From the data in Table 1 we might expect that the disparity of abilities would create considerable difficulty for most teaching methods which stress a one-step-at-a-time incremental approach and require mastery before proceeding to the next step. Boredom and withdrawal might be anticipated with the more experienced students, while the setting of a quickened pace might discourage beginners. Such disparities need not represent a serious problem for the ACT Approach, since it provides what Krashen has termed abundant "comprehensible input"[144] combined with a motivating and non-stressful atmosphere. That is to say, the more advanced students can receive ample interesting and engaging linguistic input as well as plentiful opportunities for active, expressive involvement. At the same time, beginning students can learn to comprehend the new language input and thus be rewarded, even though they cannot use the new language as actively and expressively as the more advanced students.

• Pre-Testing

All students were pre-tested in at least one modality. All students were given an oral pre-test. To four students who were available for additional pre-testing and who had received either some previous formal instruction in German or had been stationed for four or more years in Germany, the standard Defense Language Proficiency Test (DLPT), was administered, a test developed by the Defense Language Institute in Monterey, California, consisting of a taped listening comprehension section and a reading comprehension section. Two students, however, who had studied two years of German in college, who had had no significant assignment time in Germany, were not available for the DLPT. The remaining six students did not take the DLPT as a pre-test since they reported no previous instruction in German and no significant assignment time in Germany. (The results of the pre-test are displayed later in this chapter together with the post-test results.)

• Course Format

The course consisted of classes Monday through Friday, 9-12; and 1:30-4:30 (six 50-minute periods daily), for four weeks. There was one holiday, and the final Friday was used for testing. Thus, the total instructional time was 18 days (108 hours).

• Course Materials

Three different types of materials were used:

▸ An unpublished set of German materials based on the Total Physical Response Approach developed by James Asher. This material provided stimulation and activities for demonstrating comprehension through non-verbal responses for the initial semi-silent period of the first four days.

▶ An unpublished set of German materials especially created for the ACT Approach. These materials consisted of a set of dramatic "acts" approximately 500 words each in length, and they were used for days 5-9.

▶ An adaptation for tHe ACT Approach of the "German Functional Program," originally prepared by the Defense Language Institute. These materials consisted of short dialogs concerning military situations. Originally written as a basis for audio-lingual drilling, they were here taken in groups of five and re-cast as one long dramatic sequence for the ACT musical presentation described later below. They then served as the basis for role-playing activities.

● The Instructional Environment

The instructional atmosphere is, as discussed in Chapter 4, an important factor in the ACT Approach. The physical and psychological environment is believed to carry potent suggestive messages to the student. The objective here was to suggest (largely sub-consciously) to students that this was a stimulating, supportive, encouraging learning environment which would not confirm previously held negative, self-limiting attitudes about themselves or about learning. Thus, it might become an environment in which they could succeed as well as enjoy learning.

▶ Physical Setting

Since the average classroom often manifests an institutional barrenness and sameness which might easily suggest and reinforce routineness and low expectations, regular attention was given towards enhancing the quality of the classroom, as this factor was believed to significantly affect the attitude of the students. Most teachers have limited control of their learning environment. The setting of this pilot course was no exception, since the classroom was located in a converted WW II army barracks. There were supporting columns in the middle of the room, potentially obstructing the visual field. The floor was linoleum, and the fluorescent lights buzzed audibly. A number of changes were made in an effort to improve the setting:

➥ Traditional desks were replaced with comfortable chairs equipped with arm and headrests. Part of the purpose was to provide a psychologically disarming effect on students. Upon arrival, they would see a semi-circle of inviting, comfortable chairs instead of the normal classroom variety.

➥ Rugs were brought in for the floor.

➥ Noisy, humming or flickering neon bulbs were replaced. (Ideally, fluorescent lighting might be replaced with full-spectrum lighting.)

➥ Easels, large paper pads and colorful markers replaced chalkboards.

➥ A portable stereo system with cassette player was brought in. In addition to using music for the concert presentations of new material, music of different types was played for varying purposes, e.g. cheerful, delightful "wake-up" music before class began, or steady, relaxing baroque music at a scarcely audible volume during most class activities.

➥ Colorful posters and maps related to subject matter were placed on the walls and changed regularly.

The physical environment for the pilot program was given as much attention as was practical and feasible before the first class began. Theoretically, the most potent moments are those when first impressions and expectations are being subconsciously formed. The objective here was to orchestrate a set of positive impressions suggesting that the learning experience in this class would be special and positively different, impressions which could later be continuously reinforced.

▸ Psychological Setting and Psychological Means

The physical setting is considered to be an aspect of the psychological setting, insofar as it creates, affects or reinforces a person's attitudes and beliefs. The psychological environment created by the personality and actions of the teacher is believed to be the most decisive factor in the student's learning experience.

Every contact I had with students was viewed as an opportunity to suggest positive possibilities and support a positive enhancement of the student's expectations and self-image. Contact with the instructor might, of course, serve to promote fear, stress, reinforce self-limiting beliefs, etc. Thus, I never considered myself to be an "inert" ingredient in the dynamics of the learning/communication process.

The techniques, strategies and behaviors used by an instructor to create the psychological environment might differ greatly from teacher to teacher. Some key types of behaviors and techniques I used for this course are delineated below.

▸ First Contact

Much is decided in the first contact between teacher and student through setting a tone, triggering attitudes and expectations, and building or diminishing confidence. To prepare for the first meeting, I planned and set aside time to orient myself to the experience. I used visualization techniques, visualizing myself as follows:

- ❖ as a confident, loving person,
- ❖ wishing to serve the genuine needs of each student,
- ❖ curious to know each student and speak to and contribute to the growth of his/her uniqueness,
- ❖ eager to begin relationships which might grow and become increasingly purposeful,
- ❖ eager to have fun.

I wished to meet the students filled with such images and the intent to realize them. The first eye contact, handshake, words of welcome, assurance and humorous asides were intended to communicate this visualization through the myriad of semi-conscious channels which are always sending and receiving messages between communicators.

In the case of the Fort Devens class, the first contact came unplanned. When I arrived the Friday before the first Monday of class in order to prepare the room, etc., about half the team was nearby for some reason or other. The Captain, seeing me begin to unload lots of things, told the men to assist me in carrying things up to the room. This was not the way I would have chosen to meet my students--being suddenly identified as the teacher and having them ordered to act as porters for my things. And things got worse before they got better: Up in classroom, after the men had made several trips back and forth, I made the unfortunate remark: "If you want, you can move the chairs into a semi-circle..." One of the men whipped back: "What is this 'if-you-want-to' shit! Do you want the chairs moved?" I felt stunned and caught in the act of playing word games. These men were taking orders and clearly were not there because they had chosen to be there. To pretend anything else was, in the graphic language of the team sergeant, to try to "blow smoke up their ass."

I risk repeating the profanity here, because it will help indicate what the linguistic environment was often like, a reality which many teachers have to work with regularly, a given to be creatively worked with. I quickly saw that I was not dealing with a group of conventionally mannered college students. My expectations needed quick revision. I ended my first encounter by saying thanks for the help and making a hasty retreat off to a corner by myself to take stock of the situation.

One of the most important first steps in the ACT Approach is establishing a positive rapport with the students. I had not begun auspiciously well, I thought. What I did next was, I believe, better. I used my initial interaction not as demoralizing criticism or as grounds for a reactive counter-judgment, but rather I received it as useful feedback. I was able to apply something very valuable which I had learned from Neuro-Linguistic Programming (NLP): if at first you don't succeed, don't "try, try (the same thing) again"--change what you are doing! I saw that what worked in a typical college classroom probably would not work here, and that I had been given the opportunity to discover new means for achieving educational goals. I realized that I was going to have to watch my language much more closely than with college students accustomed to wordy elaborations. These soldiers were, as I quickly discovered, clearly skeptical about words and academics. They had relatively little patience for talking "about" things; they were doers. All the better opportunity, I reasoned, for using an acquisition approach where students learn through direct experience.

▸ Guiding the Emerging Group Dynamics

A fundamental strategy of the ACT Approach is to create a dynamic, unexpectedly positive group context with new student roles, where old identifications can be left behind and new possibilities can be embraced without the drag of so much past conditioning. An added challenge in the Devens class dynamics was the previously established bonds and comradeship among team members--far beyond what one normally encounters in other classrooms. They were already a tightly established group; their loyalties were already well-formed; I was an outsider. This fact would have many implications for the program. Many behaviors, some of them almost adolescent and prank-like, seemed designed to feed and keep intact their special team spirit.

It was critical that I establish myself as soon as possible as competent, credible and trustworthy. It was important that I begin to lead an attitudinal shift and a transformation of the group consciousness away from the fixed identity sets in operation, if the ACT Approach were to succeed. I knew that the first class would be crucial.

A good opportunity to work on rapport and trust came soon: the oral pre-test that same Friday afternoon. Contrary to what one might expect from a test environment, it proved to be an excellent opportunity to make a positively suggestive contact. I was able to temporarily side-step the established group dynamics and meet the students individually. In an individual meeting the student can have the undivided attention of the teacher. The quality of that attention can lay the groundwork for later fruitful interaction. Besides collecting pre-course evaluative information, I wished to establish a positive rapport with each individual student. I met each student in an open, friendly way, shaking his hand and showing my pleasure in meeting him. I took a minute to tell him how and why I was looking forward to the course and a little bit about the unique approach to be used. I explained to him the purpose and usefulness of a pre-test: that it was simply a way of providing a basis for showing him later how much he had learned. I told him it would consist of a simple conversation and some discussion about slides which would be projected onto the screen. I then conducted the exam in a professional and congenial manner, thanked the student, assured him that he would be able do well in the class, and parted with the remark that I was looking forward to seeing him on Monday. My own impression was that students left the exam feeling assured and interested in beginning on Monday.

▶ First Day of Class

As was discussed at length in the Chapter 7, the first class is considered crucial in the ACT Approach. First impressions are powerful and hang-on persistently. Class attitudes are shaped, expectations raised or lowered, and semi-conscious beliefs and biases suspended or re-confirmed. My hope and intent before beginning a first class is that the first impressions will serve as positive anchors,[145] like well-grounded cornerstones for building trust and confidence.

My main concern with the army unit was to guide the group toward a new and different group identity, using fantasy roles, a playful attitude and activities which might arouse interest and confidence. The pre-established hierarchy of authority within this military unit presented a challenge to any restructuring of the group dynamics by a new leader. In my earlier observational visits to traditional classes at Fort Devens, I quickly saw that it was necessary to win the support and affirmation of the team sergeant, the actual role model in these teams.

If he consents to relax and participate in a playful spirit, the unspoken invitation has been given to the others. Thus, before the course began I met briefly with both the team sergeant and the chief officer, expressing my pleasure at the opportunity to work with them and sharing with them my perception about how their role model would be crucial to the success of the course. They were thus enlisted as partners in orchestrating an optimal learning environment. This alliance was, I believe, a major factor in the success of the course.

▶ **Establishing Rapport**

For the first day of class, I followed very closely the first-day model outlined in Chapter 7; that sequence worked very successfully. The biggest challenge for me was adjusting to the behavior style of this group. Finding the appropriate level of behavioral congruence and rapport with a class is a crucial matter for successful teaching. Each class has its unique behavioral profile, both collectively and individually. The challenge for the teacher, above all at the outset, is not to overreact defensively, judgmentally or authoritatively, but rather to use initial behavioral responses as useful information for guiding the group dynamics more purposefully. This is, of course, easier said than done, but I find it a valuable guiding premise. This class, composed as it was of men only, who knew each other well and who were accustomed to speak and joke with each other in language and images dominated by obscenities and vulgarities, required an effective and balanced response from me. Rather than reacting judgmentally or confrontively I attempted to use whatever came from them as raw material for transformation and refinement. I was willing to acknowledge some degree of humor in the vulgarity while the next moment turning it in another direction. I chose not to pretend that I was naively oblivious to the vulgar asides and attention-getters, nor was I impatiently offended. If I became reactive, the students would be given control; if I participated from a place of larger perspective and purpose, I could remain an effective guide.

One example among many: during the first hour of class while selecting a new name, one student said he wanted to be "Georg" (pronounced in German "gay-org") and to call him "Gay" for short. He proceeded to caricature what he considered to be homosexual gestures and speech mannerisms. Quickly assessing the situation as best I could, I decided to play--very lightly--with the situation and allow it to expand the playful atmosphere. Others picked up the opportunity, giving "Georg" more and more cues (which he loved), and in the process a rich communicative context was established where everyone was bantering, reaching for language in play, and finding it!

One unexpected and disappointing adjustment I made was to dispense with using the handpuppet I normally use as a major communication stimulating prop. I had used it with great success with many different groups of widely varying ages and life styles. The team did not take to it very well, and I attribute my lack of success here with my initial inexperience in working with a group which had such strong previously established patterns of behavior. I believe I introduced the puppet too soon (on the third or fourth day) with this class--before it had become firmly and safely enough established that a considerable level of child-like behavior was not only permissible but desirable in this particular instructional setting. When one considers the rather "macho" self-image which is frequently cultivated in the military, one can appreciate the special effort needed to guide such students into an easy contact with the child-like, playful, spontaneous and creative sides of themselves. To succeed, time was needed for the initial operating peer pressure within the group to relax so as to allow new, group-accepted behaviors to be tried. I am convinced that next time I could use a puppet effectively.

▶ **Integrating the Total Physical Response Approach(TPR)**[146]

From the very first day TPR-type activities proved to be highly effective with the class. These men are both by training and avocation physically adept and in peak condition. They came to class each day after 1 1/2 hours of physical training. Also, they were accustomed to executing physical responses upon command. These factors made the integration of TPR into the instructional program perfectly natural. The men were able to experience and demonstrate quick success in comprehending German as they executed commands in German through physical responses. I was able to increase the complexity of these commands very rapidly, so that by the fourth day a single complex command involved three verb tenses, subordinate and conditional clauses, various types of demonstratives, personal and possessive pronouns, and coordinated group interaction. The following example (an English translation is provided at the end for the reader) will give an idea of the sophisticated level of linguistic challenge that was involved. These commands were given one time only. The students had to listen to the entire sequence and then enact it. A videotaped record of these command / responses is available.

(The instructor gives the following command once only, at normal speed:)

> *In einem Moment wird Franz aufstehen und an das Fenster*
> *gehen, unter dem der Ball liegt. Er wird den Ball aufheben und dem*
> *Mann neben ihm den Ball geben. Nachdem Franz ihm den Ball gegeben*
> *hat, aber nicht vorher, wird Bodo aufstehen und an die Tafel gehen und*
> *eine Nummer zwischen 1-10 auf das Papier schreiben. Sobald er diese*
> *Nummer geschrieben hat, wird Helmut aufstehen und diese Zahl von*
> *Schritten machen--geradeaus vor sich. Wenn er den letzten Schritt*
> *gemacht hat, ruft er den Namen von einem seiner Kameraden. Wenn*
> *dieser Mann seinen Namen hört, springt er auf, läuft schnell zu der Tür,*
> *öffnet sie und holt die leere Saftdose vom Tisch im Korridor. Sobald er*
> *durch die Tür gegangen ist, springt der Mann vor der Hintertür auf und*
> *versteckt sich hinter seinem Stuhl. Wenn der Mann vom Korridor ins*
> *Zimmer zurückkommt, sieht er vier leere Stühle im Zimmer. Er wird die*
> *Dose auf einen Stuhl legen und sich auf einen anderen setzen. Wenn er*
> *sich niedersetzt, laufen alle anderen zu ihren Stühlen zurück.*

English translation of the above:

> "In a moment Franz will get up and go to the window under
> which the ball is lying. He will pick up the ball and give the ball to the man
> next to him. After Franz has given him the ball, but not before, Bodo will
> stand up and go to the chart and write a number between 1-10. As soon as
> he has written the number, Helmut will stand up and take this number of
> steps--straight ahead in front of him. When he has taken the last step he
> will call out the name of one of his team mates. When this man hears his
> name, he will jump up, run to the door, open it and fetch the empty juice
> can from the table in the corridor. As soon as he has gone through the
> door, the man in front of the rear door will stand up and hide behind his
> chair. When the man comes back from the corridor, he will see four
> empty chairs in the room. He will place the can on one of the chairs and
> sit down in another. When he sits down, all the others will run back to
> their chairs."

This command is indirect and thus requires recognition of third
person singular verb forms which are often irregular. It also contains
subordinate clauses of various types with inverted German word order,
some of them beginning with relative pronouns. The present, future and
present perfect verb tenses are used. The command involves five
persons, the identity of two of whom is not revealed until the action is
underway, thus requiring the entire class to understand all the
instructions and be prepared to become involved.

TPR activities during the first week were especially suited to this
group where the initial discrepancy in student ability was so great.
Had the focus during these first days been on spoken response, these

differences would have been glaringly apparent and might have contributed to discouragement and demoralization of the true beginners.

This and other comparably complex commands were executed with remarkable accuracy and motivation upon their first presentation after 15-18 hours of instruction. The form proved ideal in building individual confidence and competence as well as contributing to a group spirit engaged in successful collective effort. The success achieved through these activities wedded with my participation and praise helped strengthen the growing rapport and trust between me and the class.

A further advantage of integrating TPR techniques into this program is the emphasis placed on concrete objects. One of the goals of this program was to teach a large quantity of military vocabulary, much of it involving the explanation and demonstration of equipment and procedures. Making language concrete and functional as soon as possible is highly desirable, and this can be realized through TPR activities very easily. Very soon I was able to command the students to fetch the rifle, take it apart, give such and such a part to so and so and have him reassemble it in the following order, etc.

▶ The Use of Music

Music, a key ingredient in the ACT Approach, was used as discussed in Chapter 9. "Concert Presentations" were used to introduce most new material. A variation I found useful was to use a variation or a repeat of the Second or "Passive" Concert Presentation from the day before after the relaxation guided fantasy which I would begin the day with. This provided a relaxed review/reinforcement in a most economical way. In addition, slow baroque music was used as a scarcely audible background for nearly all activities. This was designed as a frame for the instructional atmosphere and to serve as a positive associational bridge from one activity or day to another.

▶ Activation Techniques: From Skits to Formal Briefings

Positive rapport and a playful spirit were successfully established during the first days, laying the groundwork for the presentation and activation techniques discussed in Chapters 9 and 10. This experimental course drew upon all these techniques, and the reader is referred to those chapters for a comprehensive discussion. The activation sequences moved naturally from comprehension activities to simple one-word voluntary responses to playful role readings and then on to simple conversational role plays, culminating in situational skits which small groups would present for each other.

The most novel activation activity for the Devens course was the "briefing"--a very common and important communication form for a soldier. It is most often an informational report and/or set of instructions concerning an existing situation and/or planned operation. The ability to conduct an accurate and comprehensible "briefing" was thus an important objective of the course.

By the middle of the third week students were giving simple briefing instructions using flipcharts, diagrams and maps. Soon they were fielding clarifying questions on the briefing, and by the beginning of the fourth week they were able to work successfully with very complex mission briefings--described in the section below on final testing.

• A Typical Day in Class

The following outline sketches the instructional pattern of a typical class day after the first four days:

➡ 8:30-9:00: Classroom ready for students: chairs arranged, posters in place, props made ready. The same music as that used in previous day's concert presentation is playing in the background, serving as an "anchor" stimulus and bridge back to previous day.[147] After preparing the room, I go to another room to spend five or ten minutes, collecting and centering myself, visualizing in my mind the successful unfolding of the day's activities.

➡ 9:00-9:15: Light, easy, friendly welcome in German; shared anecdotes, personal questions, bridging from where students are in their own internal experience to the beginning collective experience together. Rapport building.

➡ 9:15-9:30: Some form of bridging review from the previous day. This could be in the form of a guided fantasy in which the content, activities and anecdotal moments of the previous day are retold in lively images and metaphors; or, a reformulation of the previous day's content is delivered to a musical background (a variation on the second concert presentation);[148] or a metaphorical story mirroring the dynamics of the class in some way.[149]

➦ 9:30-10:00: Activation and communication activities, e.g. TPR, primary activation activities such as choral pantomiming, role-reading, songs, comprehension checks.[150]

➦ 10:00-10:10: Break

➦ 10:10-11:10: Secondary activation, e.g. role plays; skits; elaborative discussions and demonstrations involving equipment, situational challenges described or implied in the text; briefings. (The activities reflect the level of competence at that particular time.)

➦ 11:10-11:20: Break

➦ 11:20-12:20: Presentational phase of new material. Global overview, musical presentations I and II.[151]

➦ 12:20-2:00: Lunch

➦ 1:45-2:00: Room ready for return of students: props and new materials readied. Second concert music playing in background as associational anchor.

➦ 2:00-2:10: Light conversation, re-establishing rapport.

➦ 2:10-2:30: Variation on Concert II: same music, lightly varied text presentation, slightly more conversational and anecdotal in style. Students listen quietly. Instructor makes the suggestion that even if they think they are drifting or napping, they will hear and comprehend everything he says.

➦ 2:30-3:10: Primary activation, e.g. choral and individual role reading with pantomime; elaborative expansion and discussion; communication activities using pictures;[152] brief communication activities in pairs.

➦ 3:10-3:20: Break

➦ 3:20-4:10: Continued primary activation, increasing use of physical props: pictures, maps, objects, equipment for demonstration (TPR activities in beginning, then later the students accompany their demonstrations with increased spoken explanation and/or commands).

➦ 4:10-4:20: Break

•❖ 4:20-5:00: Secondary activation: skits, role plays, briefings, songs. (See Appendix 2 for a list of typical activations.)

A demanding schedule, but once good rapport, positive expectations and the flow of positive energy were created, the communica-
tion/instruction process nourished itself, and I was able to use the class as
an energy source rather than experience teaching as a drain. My goal was
to serve throughout as a unifying element, "suggesting" trustworthy pur-
posefulness and growing success, providing abundant, interesting "comprehensible input,"[153] facilitating the flow of communication, transitioning
smoothly and "seamlessly" from one activity to another, and offering
students positive, reinforcing feedback. This was, of course, a challenging
role, one which I could not expect to fill perfectly. There were days when
it was harder for me to step away from my own personal concerns to be fully
present. Students perceive (mostly unconsciously) such unevenness, and it is
in such moments that resistance and negativity has a chance to grow.
When I sensed that things were "off-track," I used the following class
break to work on some inner centering, with a clear intent to reconnect to my
own inner clarity and sense of purpose.

• The Snowball Effect of Success

Once the snowball effect of continuing success is rolling, the learning effects build rapidly. This was the expectation underlying the design
of the Devens course. This pilot class had deliberately been scheduled for
a fraction of the time allotted to the regular program's course. In the ACT
pilot course students achieved a level of competence in four weeks most
often superior to the level they or others had achieved in the regular program's 12 week (360 hour) language courses. The group's ranking officer reported that he was able to communicate better in German after four weeks
of the ACT course than he was in Czech after a full intensive _year_ of Czech
at the DLI program in Monterey. Details of the results and the means used
to determine them are reported below.

Course Evaluation

• Procedures and Tests

The following measures were used to evaluate the achievement of
the experimental program:

▶ The Defense Language Proficiency Test (DLPT)

This two-part standardized test prepared by the Defense Language Institute in Monterey, California, is used throughout armed services' language programs. The DLPT used here consisted of:

⟶ a listening comprehension measure: the student hears conversational interchanges on tape followed by oral questions on content; he must mark the most correct response on a multiple choice answer sheet.

⟶ a reading comprehension measure: the student reads short passages and marks the most appropriate response to questions on a multiple choice answer sheet. Both tests are machine scored.

▶ A Specialized Task Oral Exam (STO)

A two-part oral test (described below) was administered to each student separately following the course. Each test was video-taped and/or audio taped in its entirety. The oral test consisted of both oral comprehension and oral production measures as described below:

⟶ *An Information Gathering Exercise*

The student was asked to participate in the following scenario: he was told he would serve as a bilingual interpreter between a German-speaking native informant and an English-speaking interrogating officer. The course instructor played the role of the native informant. The director of the Fort Devens' language programs played the role of the English-speaking interrogating officer. The student was shown a series of slides depicting various types of military equipment, village scenes, and terrain. The examinee was asked to formulate questions as to the military relevance of what was depicted on the slides. The "native informant" replied at length, with a wealth of detail. The examinee was required to convert the explanations of the German "informant" accurately into English for the "officer." The examinee was allowed to ask the "native" clarifying questions, and was often instructed to ask specific questions by the "officer." Thus, the task required students to a) be able to understand a complex narrative involving factual detail; b) engage verbally with the "native," in German, in exchanges designed to clarify information, and c) translate all pertinent information into English.

∞ A Complex Task Briefing

Each student listened to the instructor give a complex mission briefing in German at normal speed. A schematic representation of the mission was referred to on a flipchart. The standard briefing lasted for approximately six minutes, without interruption. It consisted of approximately 625 words. After listening once to the briefing the student was allowed to ask clarifying questions; the number of questions never exceeded four. The student was then handed the pointer and instructed to give the identical briefing to the "visiting officer," who was played by the director of the Fort Devens' language programs.

• Scoring

▸ Listening and Reading

The DLPT for listening comprehension and reading is machine scored according to the 0-5 skill level rating scale developed by the Defense Language Institute Foreign Language Center in Monterey, California. It is comparable to the more familiar FSI rating scale used by the Foreign Service Institute. Although the DLPT is a five-number scale it may be considered a ten-unit scale, since each number has two theoretically equidistant units, i.e. 0, 0+, 1, 1+, etc. (See *Appendix* 4 for the standard description of the DLI Rating Scales.)

▸ Speaking

The oral exams, both pre- and post-tests, were evaluated and scored according to the DLI Rating Scale for listening and speaking proficiency by an independent evaluator formally trained in evaluating the FSI oral interview. The evaluator, unacquainted with the instructor or the students, was contracted to evaluate the audio tapes of the pre-test and the video tapes of the post-test.

● **Results and Discussion**

Table 2 records the pre- and post-test scores for both the DLPT and the *STO* (Specialized Task Oral Exam for Listening and Speaking).

Table 2
Test Results

Name	DLPT* Listening		DLPT Reading		STO** Listening		STO Speaking	
	Pre-	Post-	Pre-	Post-	Pre-	Post-	Pre-	Post-
M.B.	0	1	0	1+	2	2+	0+	1+
J.C.	1	2	2	2+	1	2+	1	1+
R.G.	0+	1+	1	2	2	2+	0+	1
M.H^x	#	#	#	#	#	#	#	#
J. J.	#	1	#	1	1	1	0+	1
W.M.	[0]	0+	0	0	0	1	0	1
J.M.	[0]	0+	0	1	0	1	0	1
C.P.	[0]	1	0	2	0+	1	0	1
W.R.	1	2	1	1	2+	2+	1	1+
D.T.	#	1	#	0+	0+	1+	0+	1
V.W.	#	1	#	0+	1	1+	0	1
C.W.	[0]	0	0	0+	0	1	0	0+

*	=	Defense Language Proficiency Test in German
**	=	Specialized Task Oral Exam
x	=	No post-test due to hospitalization
#	=	Unavailable for testing
[0]	=	Pre-test not taken. 0-level assumed. No previous German.

▶ Discussion

A number of DLPT pre-test scores could not be obtained because students were unavailable for testing or because the student had received no previous instruction in German. The former cases are marked with a #; for the latter cases, a score of [0] was assigned since those with no previous German instruction would necessarily score zero. All pilot program students were given the STO pre-test, and all were given both the DLPT and STO post-tests, with the exception of M.H. who was hospitalized at the time of the post-tests.

▸ DLPT Listening Comprehension

The average positive change was 1.5 units on the 10 unit (five-number) DLI scale. It can be noted that the DLPT listening comprehension scores are regularly lower than the STO listening scores. The DLPT is mechanical in nature: taped conversations are heard through ear phones. The STO, in contrast, is an authentic communication interchange utilizing the student as an active participant. Only one listening test out of nine showed no positive change. It is interesting that the one student showing no change was the youngest in the group (18), was an outsider to the team (he was still unassigned but available to take a language course), and came from a rural community in Virginia where he had never had exposure to language sophistication other than the local idiom. His confidence level was the lowest in the group. It might be expected that the impersonal, mechanical nature of the DLPT test tape could have inhibited his test performance on the listening comprehension section. It is significant that he showed a positive gain on the DLPT reading test and a full two unit gain on both sections of the STO.

▸ DLPT Reading

The average positive change between pre- and post-DLPT Reading tests was 1.62 units, slightly above the gain in listening comprehension scores. Two students, W.M. and W.R., made no positive gain on this measure, although they showed positive changes on the DLPT Listening test.

▸ STO Listening

The average pre-test score in listening comprehension on the STO test was slightly less than a one (.95) on the five-number DLI Rating Scale. The average post-test score was somewhat higher than a 1+ (1.64 where a 1+ equals 1.5). The average positive change between pre- and post-tests was 1.36 units. Two students showed no change. One of them, W.R., began the course with a significantly higher level of communicative competence than the rest of the class (he is married to a native German and had spent over four years in Germany previous to the course). He nevertheless reported to the instructor that he felt he had made great improvement in listening and speaking in the course. His belief can be partly substantiated by the 2-unit gain seen on his DLPT Listening tests. Although his DLPT Reading score did not show a similar upward shift, this might be explained by the fact that the textual reading material in the course was geared to beginning students, whereas the language input at the oral level could be more growth producing for an advanced student, since it embodied a wide linguistic range. His performance might support Krashen's hypothesis that massive, ungraded yet comprehensible input is the key to second language acquisition.[154]

▶ STO Speaking

The average score in speaking on the STO pre-test was below a 0+ (.36) on the five-number DLI Rating Scale. The average post-test score was slightly above a 1 (1.1). The average positive change between pre- and post-tests was 1.45 units. All students showed a measurable speaking gain on the DLI Rating Scale. This is particularly noteworthy in view of the fact that the course lasted only 18 days and that the speaking skill is generally recognized as the slowest to emerge.

It was unexpected that the positive gain in speaking was higher than the gain in listening comprehension, since the receptive skills develop earlier than the expressive skills and provide the foundation for the latter. As was mentioned earlier, the majority of the class had spent varying amounts of time on assignment in Germany with an accompanying degree of passive language exposure so as to explain the higher pre-test scores in listening comprehension. Thus, the higher gain factor in speaking may simply reflect that the pre-test scores in listening were already unusually high for a "beginning" course, resulting in a lower comparative gain between pre- and post-tests than in the case of speaking performance where the pre-test scores were more uniformly low.

Perhaps the most noteworthy accomplishment of the course is the rapid achievement of speaking proficiency measurable with a standardized instrument. Few foreign language programs achieve measurable, uniformly positive results in authentic communicative competence in speaking during the first level of their program. The fact that all students except one in the Devens pilot program reached a level one or better in speaking on the standard DLI Rating Scale in an 18-day course strongly suggests that the ACT Approach was an effective means for advancing rapidly toward communicative competence.

▶ Other

Another positive implication of this project is the model it offers for working effectively with widely varying skill levels. In this class where the disparity in pre-test levels ranged from 0-2+, all students showed gains of between one and two units as a result of the course. The two students who showed no post-test gains in listening comprehension demonstrated positive changes in speaking. The ACT Approach offers programs with considerable skill-level discrepancies a model and a set of strategies to maximize positive group dynamics and the the cross-fertilization opportunities in heterogeneous situations.

• Comparing the Experimental Course with Regular Devens German Courses

Comparisons between the experimental pilot class and the data from the four previous German courses offered at Fort Devens in the regular Special Forces FL program offer additional results of considerable interest. It should be kept in mind that the regular courses used an audio-lingual drill approach and lasted 12 weeks (60 days, 360 hours) as compared to the pilot course which lasted three and a half weeks (18 days, 108 hours). Students in the four regular program courses took the DLPT Listening and Reading tests following the completion of the respective courses. No pre-tests were given to regular program classes, but a comparison of post-course scores is possible.

▸ Comparing the Achievement of Course Objectives

The stated course objective for all courses was to assist students to achieve a level of 1 on the DLI Rating Scale in listening comprehension, reading, and speaking. (See Appendix 5 for standard description of the DLI Rating Scales.)

Table 3 displays the comparison between regular and experimental program in achieving course objectives.

Table 3		
Students Achieving a Level 1 or Better		
	Regular	Pilot
DLPT Listening	26 %	73%
DLPT Reading	28%	64%

Of regular program students, 26% achieved level 1 or better on the DLPT listening comprehension and 28% a 1 or better in reading, whereas 73% of the pilot program students achieved a 1 or better on the DLPT listening comprehension and 64% a 1 or better in reading. The regular classes were not given a Specialized Task Oral Exam (STO) comparable to the one administered to the pilot program. It is not possible to say how many regular program students might have achieved the course objective of level 1 in speaking. However, speaking skills are seldom at a higher level than listening skills. Thus, we could not expect speaking performance to significantly exceed what was reported on the DLPT listening tests of the the regular program students. In the pilot program the course objective of attaining a level one or better in speaking was achieved by all students but one, C.W., who rated a 0+.

‣ Comparing the DLPT Scores

Table 4 depicts the comparison between regular and pilot programs on the DLPT Listening and Reading measures, administered upon completion of the respective courses.

Table 4 Comparison of Pilot Program to Regular Classes					
Rating	Regular Program	Pilot Program	Rating	Regular Program	Pilot Program
DLPT Listen.	%	%	DLPT Reading	%	%
0	62	8	0	62	8
0+	15	17	0+	15	25
1	18	42	1	21	33
1+	3	17	1+	3	17
2	6	17	2	0	17
Above 2	3	0	Above 2	6	8

▶ Discussion

In the four previous regular German classes 19 out of 34 students scored 0 on the DLPT Listening post test as opposed to 1 pilot course student out of 11. Results in reading were similar: 20 out of 34 students in the regular program scored 0 on the DLPT Reading post test as compared to 1 student out of 11 in the pilot course.

Thus, on DLPT Listening and Reading tests, over half the students in the regular courses demonstrated no measurable accomplishment in German, whereas only one student out of 11 in the experimental course showed no measurable gain on these tests.

The above results point to the superiority of the pilot program over previous classes in achieving the language program objective--that is, achieving a level 1 or better in listening, reading and speaking as measured on the DLI Rating Scale. Most noteworthy is the fact that the pilot program's results were obtained in slightly less than 1/3 the time spent in the regular program.

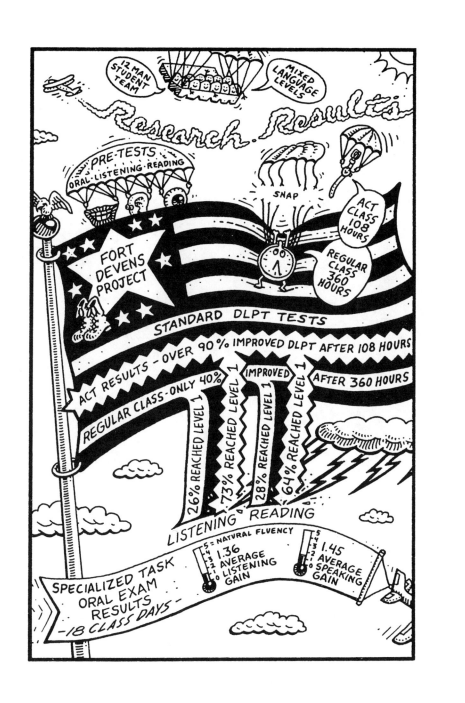

CHAPTER 14

TESTING
Some Personal Thoughts on Its Use and Abuse

Testing to Demonstrate Course Effectiveness

I am very uncomfortable with our culture's "test" mentality. In writing this book I knew that offering my readers clear, objective evidence that the ACT Approach has "proven" successful would argue persuasively for its merit. Chapters 12 and 13 do offer such evidence. Yes, it is possible for the ACT teacher to test, to produce "data," to "prove" effectiveness. And, I am glad to be able to provide interested teachers with helpful support.

Yet, as Jean Houston has noted, we have deified efficiency and quantification, and

> have found our basic metaphors in the machine and the computer.
> The result is distance, the worshipping of facts and products that can be evaluated and held constant at a time of radical change, rather than risking the challenge of process and the evocation of the full potential of the brain.
> . . . This disaster has been compounded recently by standardized testing, with its reliance on a multiple-choice format that asks the test-taker to select *the* correct answer from a limited number of alternatives. The more complex but academically less efficient challenge to come up with an

original response is not possible in the present Reign of Quantity, and our model of the brain seems to have become that of a primitive and rather inadequate computer.[155]

Thus, fundamentally, I do not wish either to reinforce or contribute to what I consider a misguided preoccupation with testing and evaluation. I *do* wish to contribute to a revitalization of the learning experience, enabling students to rediscover the joy and excitement of authentic learning, rather than learning to please the teacher or to pass the test. And, I do wish to contribute to the revitalization of the teaching experience. My fellow teachers deserve the opportunity to know the fulfillment and delight which can come as we open, risk and express much more of ourselves in the classroom.

The desire for credible evidence that one's teaching is good and effective, perhaps even more effective than some other way, is understandable and very human. But to believe that we need "data" before we can know if we are succeeding is dangerous. I sense that the more we bow to the test god, the more we undermine our personal and deepest confidence--a confidence which lies at the heart of our well-being. As teachers we simply *know* when our teaching is vitally connected to the growth of our students and ourselves. No test will actually prove whether this vital link is present or not. If we lose our self-trust, we will surely lose the students' trust as well. After embarking on the ACT Approach ten years ago, I "knew" I had discovered something wonderful and that many other teachers and students would rejoice when they "knew" the same thing. I also knew that in order to communicate what I "knew," I needed to communicate my excitement in a language which could be understood and accepted. Thus, I used standardized tests and the Oral Proficiency Interview at the end of my courses to document the effectiveness of the program.

On the one hand, the results have been gratifying: colleagues approve and are often grateful; some can now justify their own implementation of ACT principles to administrators or colleagues, because of "supportive data." Other colleagues approve for different reasons. The data facilitates the belief that they now "know" and "understand" what I am doing. They usually find "it" "interesting," another ubiquitous academic euphemism which might be translated more honestly as:

> *I don't really know what to say about 'it'; I don't feel confident or bold enough to dispute 'it'; I don't feel confident or bold enough to endorse 'it'; so why don't we let 'it' go at that.*

All in all, the "data" of Chapters 12 and 13 have made the acceptance of this book and the acceptance of ACT easier.

Other Ways of Knowing about Course Effectiveness

The "supportive data" of Chapters 12 and 13 notwithstanding, I would like to say unequivocally that my authority to advocate the ACT Approach is not based upon any set of "empirical data." The great success of the program lies in phenomena I will never be able to test empirically. I am speaking of my daily experiences during hundreds of hours of class with students as they delight in learning, as they transform over the course of twelve weeks from mute, self-conscious strangers to confident, expressive, authentic communicators in German. I am speaking of "Else" (her new German identity) who came to me half way through the class. She reported that the course had given her the self-confidence and inner strength finally to quit smoking. She wasn't exactly sure how or why, but the class had somehow provided her with an environment where she could feel good about helping herself realize other goals which had previously eluded her.

How could I "prove" that the class had anything to do with Else's breakthrough? Still, I "know"--in a way that test data could never speak to me--I know at my deepest gut-level that the ACT "experience" is an invitation to positive transformation, an environment which supports such transformation. I see it happen in each and every course. The students themselves give the best testimony. (See examples of the three student evaluations reproduced in Chapter 12.)

Testing and Homework to Produce Grades

As I mentioned earlier, I have seen some usefulness in providing test data about the effectiveness of the ACT Approach. Thus, I have administered standardized tests and oral proficiency interviews upon the completion of the course.

Another question, however, is whether to test students throughout the course as part of a strategy to assign them a "grade."

But for whom is the grading process geared? In the service of what? These are troubling questions for me. The issue of testing in an acquisition-based approach is very sensitive. My colleagues are clearly uneasy as well. Krashen and Terrell open their chapter on testing with concerns echoing my own:

> . . . language acquisition is a subconscious process, dependent on two fac-
> tors: the amount of comprehensible input the students get, and the
> strength of their affective filters, that is the amount of input the students
> "allow in." [see Chapter 3 for my discussion of "comprehensible input"
> and "affective filters".] It is, thus, in a sense, unfair to grade students on
> the amount of target language they acquire since it is up to the instructor
> to provide the input, at least in class, and since the strength of the filter is
> beyond their conscious control. Rather, **it could be argued that we
> should only grade on factors such as attendance and
> participation.**[156](emphasis mine)

Although Krashen and Terrell see the illogic in testing the student's level of acquisition to determine his grade (since the essence of the
acquisition process is out of his conscious control), nevertheless, they bow to
the pressure of the test/grade mentality mentioned in the earlier paragraphs above and later describe a number of testing strategies they use in
the Natural Approach.[157] I have sympathy for their inconsistency, since I,
too, have tested my students against my better judgment for many years.

• An Experiment with More Homework and Tests

Even after the excellent learning experiences achieved in my first
ACT course where I assigned no homework and gave no tests except the
post-course standardized MLA exam, I wavered in my conviction that testing would have a deleterious effect in the ACT Approach. I rationalized
that if students did as well as they did without homework and tests, they
would probably do even better if they spent more time outside class with
the course material (homework) and also, if they reviewed and reinforced
the material in preparation for tests. I further reasoned that homework
and tests would give me a more "acceptable" rationale for assigning a
grade and giving credit for the course. Thus, in subsequent years, I began
experimenting with varying amounts of homework and testing.

The residual "traditional" teacher in me was delighted with the
willing acceptance by the highly motivated ACT students of nearly any
amount of homework--for a while. I took advantage of the early enthusiasm and willingness, pushing them as far as they could go. I began to ask
for three to four hours of homework each night. I reasoned that if students
were to supplement the rich, sub-conscious *acquisition* environment of the
ACT classroom with an equal amount of conscious *learning*, the results
would no doubt be spectacular.

The actual results were sobering. After several weeks, the signs of
student burn-out were unmistakable. Fatigue I had never seen before began
appearing in classes. It was as if a saturation level had been reached, as if

they were starting to "drown" in German. Also, I began to notice indirect signs of resistance to me personally--avoidance during the social breaks, unwilling eye contact. However, I was "invested" in my result-oriented strategy to the point that I chose to ignore these non-verbal signals. Finally, one student approached me after class and "unloaded." He was feeling overwhelmed, exhausted, unmotivated, and he knew others were feeling similarly. They felt very unhappy about their change of attitude, since they had all loved the class so much, but something had changed. Class was becoming a grind.

Finally, I got the message. Suddenly, so much of what I had worked for, an atmosphere of delight, safety, and easy risk, of motivating successes and confidence-building feedback, all leading to remarkable communicative competence in a short time--all this was being sabotaged. Not by my students, but by my own slide back into a traditional work-ethic, an ethic I assumed I had broken through.

During this same period of more homework, I began giving comprehensive weekly tests. Since I had been assigning grammar, exercises and reading in the hopes of more conscious mastery, I felt justified in testing and grading these same exercises.

Again, my intentions backfired. Initially, I got the conscious mastery I had hoped for. Students digested the material to the extent possible in conscious learning. They memorized, applied rules, and as long as the test examples mirrored class exercises, learning was achieved. The disappointment was the same as I had experienced for years in my traditional language classes: just like the multitude of students in traditional classes, my students could learn the rules and pass a test on them, but they failed to apply the rules in authentic speaking contexts. My intent to wed and synchronize conscious learning and unconscious acquisition strategies was simply not working. I had to ask myself about the quality of "learning" the students had obtained through conscious memorization. Was passing a test actually a superficial varnish that could convince someone that something valuable had been accomplished, when, in actuality, there was little carry-over of "learned" material into actual expression of these skills? How many hundreds of "tests" had I taken in my years of schooling, only to forget the content shortly after?

A further "cost" of the increased testing was a psychological one. Since the tests had "grades," students inevitably began to focus upon them. Intense preparation for the tests became the practice. Once the test was over, the class let down and showed a marked drop in motivation. And, as the tests became more and more central to the course, the quality of the in-class experience deteriorated substantially. Tests, more symbolic, abstract, and removed from the experience of the moment, were utterly different from the classroom experience I had worked so hard to develop. To my own dismay, my efforts and the experiences of my students began to resemble more and more a traditional language learning experience. We all were the unhappier for it.

It was at the conclusion of such a class, in the spring of 1983, that I received the invitation to conduct an ACT German course for the U.S. Army at Fort Devens. It was also after my first experience reading Krashen's theory of second language acquisition. The army course provided me with an opportunity to try a radically different alternative to the weakened, compromised version of the ACT model I had just finished with university students. For the army course I resolved to assign no homework, do no formal grammar study, and give no tests, except for the final standardized test required by the project. The results were the best I had ever achieved – both subjectively and objectively. The tests demonstrated conclusive, significant acquisition, and the students remained delighted with the experience from start to finish.

I now knew more: acquisition results were the most satisfying results, both for students and teacher, and they were best achieved with minimal conscious "learning" activities. I now had the experiences I needed to justify taking acquisition theory seriously. I no longer felt compelled to "cover my tracks" by giving homework and tests to the same extent.

Now in my ACT classes I still assign homework, not in an attempt to "push" students and force "learning" but in the spirit and context described in Chapter 11 under "Homework," in the attempt to enjoyably enrich the comprehensive ACT experience.

Some Concluding Thoughts on Our Obsession with Testing

We live in a cultural era obsessed with testing, judging, measuring, evaluating, and demonstrating. The sister obsession to testing is "data." If what one does is not accompanied by "test data" it is suspect, and may often be dismissed. Academic credibility, respectability, and reliability have become practically synonymous with such "data."

Our obsession affects teachers and students alike. My own high school children considered school a kind of ordeal, a rite of passage through P-SAT's, SAT prep tests, SAT prep courses, followed by the actual SAT's, and the concomitant elation or despair when the scores arrived. All this with assorted other state and local standardized testing along the way. Some of their teachers' pleading notwithstanding, it seemed obvious to them that their test scores were what really mattered--to the school, to their peers, to the college admissions committees. Test scores together with their grades, also earned through tests.

Not all children cope successfully with our insistent testing. One of my own children illustrated this point poignantly and was rescued from failure mostly by luck. He has great difficulty with writing and sequential tasks. For him, tests were particularly difficult, especially on his self-esteem. He began to withdraw from school work and deliberately flunked out of high school. After an agonizing search for alternatives, we finally discovered a high school for the arts. In this setting my son's other "intelligences" (spatial, kinesthetic, musical)[158] were stimulated and encouraged. He was "tested"--but not *about* art, music, theater production and acting. His tests in these areas came though actual doing, performing, and cooperating in joint projects. Most schools offer arts and courses which challenge more than what Gardner calls our "linguistic" and "logico-mathematical intelligences." But these courses are supplementary "enrichments." They do not figure into the "bottom line." My son finished high school having acquired many skills, having learned much through experience--feeling good about himself and his abilities.

My son was then admitted to an unusual and highly selective university program in technical theater on the basis of his portfolio, his experiential record, and his person. The admissions committee-one of the few such in the country--purposely did not request SAT scores. My son's story has a happy ending. There are countless others who are not so fortunate. Most of us know young persons who leave high school feeling like failures, expressing anger, depression, resignation, or escape into any number of self-destructive paths.

The pressure for test results is no less destructive for teachers and administrators. It blinds us to our true mission of liberating and encouraging the wondrous potential each individual possesses. Instead, we feel driven to produce "data." And, a subtle adjustment of priorities follows. We find ourselves bowing to the will of the test god. We speak what it wants to hear and train our initiates in the dogma of acceptance. Even in my own case, in spite of what I have come to know deep inside as well as through my senses (watching my students delight in learning and become competent and self-confident at the same time)--knowing all that, I still experience moments of doubt, I still feel the pressures of the test god and wish I had some more "data."

The testing pressure reaches beyond the teacher's anxiety about his/her students' comparative scores. A colleague recently shared with me the story of an elementary school principal who had actually been falsifying students' scores on the state's standardized test over a period of years in an attempt to avoid a supervisor's critical scrutiny. As a result, her health and career were ruined.

In sum, I am learning to trust what I experience immediately as I use the ACT Approach. I see that my students are motivated to reach for excellence because they are succeeding and they want even more success. They are enjoying learning; they are playful, spontaneous and creative. After leaving my classes, most search for ways to continue their German experience, either by taking more courses or traveling to Germany. I am getting the results I had always dreamed of: happy, successful, motivated, and competent students. When I am able to keep this fact in my consciousness I am able to put "testing" in better perspective: it is a useful tool to demonstrate certain accomplishments to those outside the immediate experience, to those who don't have the benefit of the eyes, ears, hearts and minds of ourselves and our students. For the latter we don't need many tests. For the others we need far fewer than we believe.

Let us teach so as to free the potential of our students and ourselves--with joy, with great heart, with a keen mind, and playful seriousness. Then let us decide how to "test".

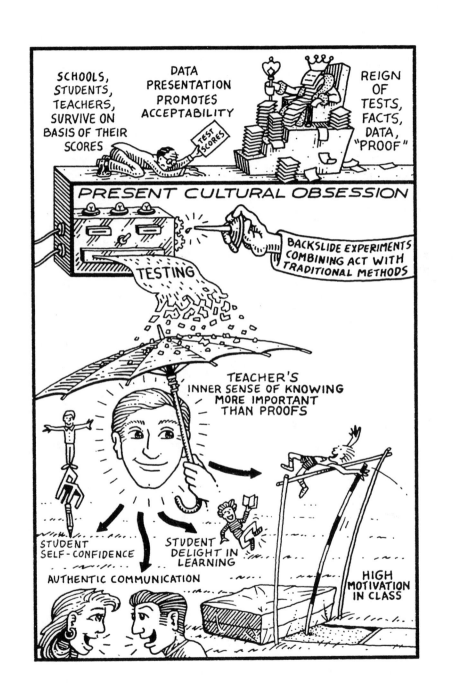

Appendix 1

Eine Deutsche Reise
(A German Journey)
by Charles Schmid and Lynn Dhority

WOLLEN IST KÖNNEN
(Wanting to is being able to)

Personen	Characters
Die Dame	Lady
Der Junge	Boy
Die Flugbegleiterin	Flight Attendant (female)
Der Flugbegleiter	Flight Attendant (male)
Der Mann	Man
Die Mutter	Mother
Das Baby	Baby
Der Pilot	Pilot

Erster Akt

Die Ankunft

	First Act
	The Arrival

Im Flugzeug.	In the plane.
Es ist elf Uhr morgens.	It's eleven o'clock in the morning.
Das Flugzeug fliegt durch die Wolken.	The plane is flying through the clouds.
Sie sind rosa und golden.	They are pink and gold.
Und da kommt die Sonne!	And there comes the sun!

—1—

Dame	Fräulein, einen Kaffee, bitte.	Miss, a coffee, please.
Flug-begleiterin	Einen Kaffee für die gnädige Frau. Mit Milch oder ohne Milch?	A coffee for the gracious lady. With or without milk?
Dame	Mit Milch, bitte.	With milk, please.
Fl. Begl.	Mit Milch, gut. Und Sie, junger Mann? Was möchten Sie trinken?	With milk, fine. And you, young man? What would you like to drink?

Junge	Bringen Sie mir, bitte, eine Tasse Tee. Mit Zitrone. Vielen Dank!	Bring me, please, a cup of tea. With lemon. Many thanks!
Fl. Begl.	Sehr schön. Mit Zitrone. *(sie geht)*	Very good. With lemon. *(she goes)*

—— 2 ——

Die Dame sieht aus dem Fenster. Sie lächelt.

The lady is looking out the window. She is smiling.

Junge	Sie fliegen zum ersten Mal, nicht wahr?	You're flying for the first time, aren't you?
Dame	*(sehr überrascht)* Ja, das stimmt. Aber, woher wissen Sie, daß es das erste Mal ist?	*(very surprised)* Yes, that's right. But how do you know that it's the first time?
Junge	Ich weiß nicht. Ich spüre es.	I don't know. I sense it.
Dame	Ja, Sie haben recht. Aber wie spüren Sie das?	Yes, you're right. But how do you feel that?
Junge	Es ist eigentlich nicht schwer. Es ist sogar einfach. Sie sehen immer aus dem Fenster. Und Sie lächeln immer.	It's actually not difficult. It's easy in fact. You're always looking out the window. And you're always smiling.
	(sie lachen zusammen)	*(they laugh together)*
Junge	Aber Sie sind ein bißchen nervös. Entspannen Sie sich! Es ist leicht, sich zu entspannen. Machen Sie die Augen zu! Und jetzt: einatmen, langsam ausatmen.	But you are a bit nervous. Relax! It's easy to relax. Close your eyes! And now: inhale, slowly exhale.

Dame	(*Sie atmet ein und aus*)	(*She breathes in and out*)
	Danke.	Thanks.
	Jetzt geht's viel besser.	Yes, now it's much better.
	Sie sind ein sympatischer junger	You are a nice
	Mann.	young man.
	Wie heißen Sie denn?	So what's your name?

Junge	Ich heiße Marko.	My name is Marko.

Dame	Es freut mich sehr, Marko.	Pleased to meet you, Marko.
	Und ich heiße Maria Häuser.	And my name is Maria Häuser.

Marko	Freut mich auch, Frau Häuser.	Pleased to meet you, too, Mrs.
	Haben Sie Kinder?	Häuser.
		Do you have children?

Maria	Haben Sie meinen Ehering	Did you see my wedding ring?
	gesehen?	

Marko	Ja, ich habe Ihren Ring gleich	Yes, I saw your ring immediately.
	gesehen.	

Maria	Meine Güte!	My goodness!
	Sie sind sehr aufmerksam.	You are very observant.
	Wie alt sind Sie?	How old are you?

Marko	Raten Sie mal!	Just guess!

Maria	Na ja, ich weiß nicht.	Well, uh, I don't know.
	Dreizehn, vierzehn, fünfzehn?	Thirteen, fourteen, fifteen?

Marko	(*Marko lacht.*)	(*Marko laughs.*)
	Nein, noch nicht.	No, not yet.

Maria	Also, sind Sie zwölf?	Well, are you twelve?

Marko	Noch nicht.	Not yet.
	Ich bin eigentlich elf Jahre	I am actually eleven years
	alt.	old.
	Also, bitte, sagen Sie "du" zu mir.	Well, please, call me (by)
		"du".

—— 3 ——

Fl. Begl.	(*Der Flugbegleiter fragt:*) Möchten Sie etwas lesen?	Would you like something to read?

| Maria | Was haben Sie denn zu lesen? | What do you have to read? |

| Fl. Begl. | Wir haben Illustrierte und Zeitungen. | We have picture magazines and newspapers. |

| Maria | Haben Sie englische oder amerikanische Zeitungen? | Do you have English or American newspapers? |

| Fl. Begl. | Leider nicht. Wir haben keine Zeitungen auf englisch. | Unfortunately not. We have no newspapers in English. |

| Maria | Danke. Ich möchte etwas auf englisch lesen. | Thanks. I'd like something to read in English. |

| Marko | Ich habe ewas auf englisch für Sie. | I have something in English for you. |

| Maria | Tatsächlich? | Really? |

| Marko | Einen Augenblick. Ich werde es holen. | One moment. I'll fetch it. |

(Marko geht nach hinten und bringt ein Buch zurück.)   *(Marko goes to the rear and brings back a book.)*

Da haben Sie etwas Schönes zu lesen. Auf englisch und auf deutsch.

There you have something nice to read. In English and in German.

| Maria | Wie heißt das Buch? | What's the book called? |

| Marko | Es heißt *Aphorisms of the World* or *Aphorismen aus der ganzen Welt*. | It's called .... or *Aphorisms from the Whole World*. |

| Maria | Vielen Dank. Ich habe es verstanden. Also du verstehst und liest Englisch. | Many thanks. I understood it. So you understand and read English. |

| Marko | Ja, natürlich. Mein Vater ist Englischlehrer. Meine Mutter ist Französin. Ich habe auch eine Schwester, einen Bruder, einen Hund und eine Katze. | Yes, of course. My father is an English teacher. My mother is French. I also have a sister, a brother, a dog and a cat. |

	Wir sprechen oft Englisch zu Hause.	We often speak English at home.
	Sprachen sind eigentlich leicht zu lernen.	Languages are actually easy to learn.
	Und es macht viel Spaß, eine neue Sprache zu lernen.	And it's fun learning a new language.
	Alles geht leicht, wenn man daran glaubt.	Everything is (goes) easy, if one believes in it.
Maria	Ja, das stimmt. Kannst du andere Sprachen sprechen?	Yes, that's right. Can you speak other languages?
Marko	Ja, Deutsch und Englisch und nur ein bißchen Französisch und Italienisch. Ich bin noch sehr jung, wissen Sie.	Yes, German and English and only a bit of French and Italian. I am still very young, you know.
Maria	Das ist ja großartig!	But that's terrific!
Marko	Aber ich kann noch nicht Englisch schreiben. Hier im Buch ist ein Zitat von Goethe. "Disziplin bringt Freiheit." Und er hat recht. Er meint natürlich Selbstdisziplin.	But I can't yet write English. Here in the book is a quote by Goethe. "Discipline brings freedom." And he's right. He means, of course, self-discipline.
Maria	Ja, leicht gesagt. Aber "Wollen ist Können." Kennst du diesen Denkspruch?	Yes, easier said than done. But wanting to is being able to. Do you know this saying?
Marko	Nein, gar nicht. Aber er ist prima! Und es stimmt auch. Und Schiller, der große Dichter, sagt: "Beim Spielen lernt man schnell."	No, not at all. But it's far-out! And it's right, too. And Schiller, the great poet, says: "At play one learns quickly."

—— 4 ——

Marko	Was sind Sie von Beruf?	What is your profession?
Maria	Ich bin Ärztin.	I'm a doctor (M.D..)

Marko	Ich weiß den Beruf von vielen Leuten hier im Flugzeug.	I know the profession of many people here in the plane.
Maria	Ja, zum Beispiel?	Well, for example?
Marko	Na ja, der Mann da rechts. Er ist Rechtsanwalt. Er ist noch ledig, und er fährt nach Graz. Er will seine Tante und seinen Onkel besuchen. Und die Frau drüben links ... sie ist Krankenschwester. Sie ist verheiratet. Sie hat drei Kinder: einen Sohn und zwei Töchter.	Well, the man there on the right. He's a lawyer. He's still single, and he's travelling to Graz. He wants to visit his aunt and his uncle And the woman there on the left... she's a nurse. She's married. She has three children: one son and two daughters.
Maria	Du vergißt aber nichts.	You forget (really) nothing.

—— 5 ——

	(Der Pilot unterbricht.)	*(The pilot interrupts.)*
Pilot	Meine Damen und Herren, wir haben jetzt einige atmosphärische Störungen. Bitte, schnallen Sie sich an! Es wird nicht lange dauern. Danke.	Ladies and gentlemen, we are now having some atmospheric disturbances. Please fasten your seat belts! It won't last long. Thank you.
Maria	Meine Güte! Ich fahre lieber mit der Eisenbahn. Gibt es immer atmosphärische Störungen?	My Goodness! I travel preferaby with the train. Are there always atmospheric disturbances?
Marko	Nein, nicht immer. Einen Augenblick. Das kleine Kind da weint. Entschuldigen Sie, bitte.	No, not always. One moment. That little baby there is crying. Excuse me, please.

—— 6 ——

| | *(Marko setzt sich neben die Frau mit dem Kind.)* | *(Marko sits down next to the woman with the child.)* |
| Marko | Komm, mein Kleiner, weine nicht. | Come on, my little one, don't cry. |

Schlaf, Kindchen, schlaf. | Sleep, little baby, sleep.
Der Vater hüt' | The father is tending
die Schaf. | the sheep.
Die Mutter schüttelt's | The mother is shaking the
Bäumelein. | little tree.
Da fällt herab ein Träumelein. | A little dream falls down.
Schlaf, Kindchen, schlaf. | Sleep, little baby, sleep.
(Das Kind wird tatsächlich ruhig.) | *(The child actually becomes quiet.)*

Mutter   Vielen Dank. | Many thanks.
Das ist aber sehr nett | That is really very nice
von dir. | of you.

Marko   Nichts zu danken. | You're welcome.
Ich glaube er oder sie | I think he or she
schläft jetzt. | is sleeping now.

Mutter   Es ist ein Mädchen. | It's a girl.
Nochmals, vielen Dank. | Once again, many thanks.

(Marko geht zurück zu Maria.) | *(Marko goes back to Maria.)*

Maria   Marko, du hast ein gutes Herz. | Marko, you have a good heart.

Marko   *(etwas verlegen)* | *(somewhat embarrassed)*
Entschuldigen Sie. | Excuse me.
Ich laufe jetzt | I'm going to walk
ein wenig herum. | around a bit.

Maria   Auf Wiederschauen, Marko. | Goodbye, Marko.

—— 7 ——

(Marko geht nach hinten und sieht | *(Marko goes to the rear and sees a*
einen freien Platz.) | *free seat.)*

Marko   Ist dieser Platz frei? | Is this seat free?

Mann   Ja. Bitte, setzen Sie sich. | Yes. Please sit down.
(Marko setzt sich.) | *(Marko sits down.)*
Ich heiße Jürgen Weiss. | My name is Jürgen Weiss.
Und wie heißen Sie? | And what's your name?

Marko   Ich heiße Marko Polo. | My name is Marko Polo.

Jürg.   Tatsächlich? | Really?
Also, Sie sind Abenteurer? | So, you're an adventurer?
Das ist ja interessant. | That's really interesting.

	Sie fliegen nach Wien, nicht wahr?	You're flying to Vienna, right?
Marko	Ja, richtig.	Yes, correct.
Jürg.	Und was werden Sie in Wien machen?	And what will you do in Vienna?
Marko	Ich werde meine Tante und meinen Onkel besuchen.	I'll visit my aunt and my uncle.
Jürg.	Wo wohnen Sie? Das heißt, in welchem Land?	Where do you live? That is, in which country?
Marko	Wir wohnen in Deutschland. In Stuttgart.	We live in Germany. In Stuttgart.
Jürg.	Also im Zentrum der Computerindustrie.	So, in the center of the computer industry.
Marko	Ja. Und ich liebe meinen Computer. Ich schreibe meine Hausaufgaben damit. Und Sie, Herr Weiss, Sie sind Schweizer, nicht wahr?	Yes. And I love my computer. I write my homework assignments with it. And you, Mr. Weiss, you are Swiss, aren't you?
Jürg.	Ja das stimmt. Aber woher wissen Sie das?	Yes, that's right. But how do you know that?
Marko	Sie sprechen mit einem Schweizer Akzent.	You speak with a Swiss accent.
Jürg.	Donnerwetter! Sie merken aber alles.	I'll be darned! [Thunderweather] You notice everything.

—— 8 ——

Marko	Die Menschen interessieren mich sehr, wissen Sie. Ich spreche immer mit vielen Leuten im Flugzeug.	People interest me a lot, you know. I always speak with many people in the plane.
Jürg.	Zum Beispiel?	For example?
Marko	Na ja, das Fräulein da links ist Schriftstellerin. Sie ist noch ledig.	Well, that young lady there on the left is a writer. She's still single.

Jürg.	Ich auch.	So am I.
Marko	Sehen Sie den Mann da vorne rechts?	Do you see the man there up front on the right.
Jürg.	Haben Sie schon mit ihm gesprochen?	Have you already spoken with him?
Marko	Nein, noch nicht. Aber, sehen Sie. Er macht immer Übungen mit den Füßen.	No not yet. But, look. He's always doing exercises with his feet.
Jürg.	Er ist vielleicht Turner.	He's perhaps a gymnast.
Marko	Ich glaube nicht. Seine Schultern und Arme sind zu klein. Ich glaube, er ist Tänzer.	I don't think so. His shoulders and arms are too small. I think he's a dancer.
Jürg.	Sie merken wirklich alles.	You really notice everything.
Marko	Ich interessiere mich für die Körpersprache. Wir sagen mehr mit dem Körper als mit dem Mund.	I am interested in body language. We say more with the body than with the mouth.
Jürg.	Können Sie Körpersprache verstehen?	Can you understand body language?
Marko	Ziemlich viel.	Quite a lot?
Jürg.	Ist es leicht?	Is it easy?
Marko	Eigentlich ja. Und, "Wollen ist Können."	Actually yes. And "Wanting to is being able to."
Jürg.	Fantastisch! Du bist ein echtes Wunderkind.	Fantastic! You're a real child prodigy.
Marko	Und warum fliegen Sie nach Wien?	And why are you flying to Vienna.
Jürg.	Ich bin Psychologe. Ich werde das Institut für Lernforschung besuchen.	I'm a psychologist. I'll visit the Institute for Learning-Research.

| | Sie experimentieren mit neuen Methoden. | They're experimenting with new methods. |
| | Sehr interessant. | Very interesting. |

—— 9 ——

Fl.	Da sind Sie ja!	Oh, there you are!
Begl.	Hier ist Ihr Tee mit Zitrone.	Here's your tea with lemon.
Marko	Vielen Dank.	Thanks a lot.
Fl.	*(zu Jürgen)*	*(to Jürgen)*
Begl.	Möchten Sie etwas essen oder trinken?	Would you like something to eat or drink?
Jürg	Nein, danke.	No, thanks.
	(Die Flugbegleiterin geht.)	*(The flight attendant goes.)*
Jürg.	Also, Marko, Sie sind Abenteurer und Menschenkenner.	Well, Marko, you are an adventurer and "knower of human nature".
	Was kennen Sie sonst noch?	What else do you know still?
Marko	Ich interessiere mich auch für Gedanken.	I'm also interested in thoughts.
	Denken kostet nichts und macht Spaß.	Thinking costs nothing and is fun.
	Die Gedanken sind frei.	Thoughts are free.
	Kennen Sie das Volkslied mit diesem Titel.	Do you the folksong with this title?
Jürg.	Ja, ich kenne das Lied.	Yes, I know the song.
Marko	Ich bin sehr reich, wissen Sie?	I'm very rich, you know?
Jürg	Verdient Ihr Vater so viel Geld?	Does your father earn so much money?
Marko	Nein, ich meine es nicht so.	No, I don't mean it that way.
	Ich habe alles was ich brauche.	I have everything that I need.
	Ich habe mein Leben, meinen Leib, meinen Kopf und viele wunderbare, verrückte Ideen.	I have my life, my body, my head, and many wonderful, crazy ideas.

Jürg	Ja, Marko, das stimmt.	Yes, Marko, that's right.
	Sie sind reich, sehr reich.	You are rich, very rich.

————10————

	(Die Flugbegleiterin unterbricht.)	*(The flight attendant interrupts.)*
Fl.	Meine Damen und Herren,	Ladies and gentlemen,
Begl.	wir werden in fünf	we will be landing in five minutes
	Minuten in Wien landen.	in Vienna.
	Bitte schnallen Sie sich an.	Please fasten your seat belts.
	Das Wetter in Wien ist herrlich.	The weather in Vienna is
		marvelous.
	Es ist zwölf Uhr zwanzig.	It is twelve twenty.
	Herzlich Willkommen in Wien!	A hearty welcome to Vienna!

Appendix 2

Activation Ideas
(A brief suggestive list)

Ballgames   Playfully throw a large, light (easy to catch) ball while eliciting various responses, e.g. "What's your name", "How are you", "How many....," etc. The throwing and catching (a right-brain activity) focuses attention in the kinesthetic modality, allowing the left brain to respond more freely and flexibly.

Handclapping   Especially good for learning numbers: Each student takes a number for an identity. Then a clapping rhythm is established for all to sustain. At the beginning of the rhythm cycle, the first student calls out (in rhythm) a number. The student with that number as an identity picks up the rhythm and calls out another student's number at the start of the next rhythm cycle.

New Arrival   Passport and customs scene. Use costumes and props. Have whole class divide into two's or three's and play scenes simultaneously. Then ask them to recount highlights for whole class.

Simon Says ...   This classic is always a favorite. The teacher touches a part of his body as he says: "Simon says, touch your (nose). The students touch their noses or any other body part the teacher commands <u>but only if he precedes the command with the words: "Simon says..."</u>

Changing money   A visit to the bank or change bureau. Use paper money. Have class do it simultaneously in pairs.

Puppets   Wonderful way to create playful dialogs and relationships with students. Introduce early in course. Gradually develop a biographical story for the puppet which interacts with identities of students.

Café scene	Various levels of interaction between a waiter/waitress and a couple or a single patron. Costumes and props help.
Child Prodigies	Students pretend to be at a convention of young "geniuses", playfully upstaging each other: "I am 6 years old and am a mathematician...", etc.
Card game	A favorite with students: Students assume a new identity for the game, e.g. a body part (arm elbow, etc.), a relative (aunt, nephew, etc.), a type of food, any object. Six to eight students sit in a circle on floor. Another six to eight can stand behind seated ones to act as coaches. Teacher then begins playing a card face up in front of each seated student. Teacher can do a lot of talking and naming while placing cards. As soon as a card comes up which matches another student's card, those two students try to name the identity of each other (their coaches can help). The first one to say correctly the identity of the other wins the pile of cards in front of the other. Important to guide this game lightly and playfully so that it remains "playfully" competitive.
Census Taker	Teacher or student goes around "knocking" on imaginary doors in front of students asking all kinds of delightful questions for the "census".
Daily anecdote	Students are asked to volunteer to tell an interesting, enjoyable anecdote the following day. Purpose is to entertain: a pleasure, not a chore.
Mime verbs	Verbs of current text chapter are displayed on a chart. Students spontaneously come forward and mime a verb. Others guess what it is.
Visitor from another planet	Student pretends to arrive on Earth and is amazed -- asks all kinds of questions. Other students quiz visitor.
Family Tree	As a prelude to students creating their own family tree, teacher presents his "family" in the form of "unusual" pictures (magazine cut-outs) with a remarkable accompanying story. Students can do the same in successive days.

On the Phone	Students call each other on imaginary phones, make plans, dates, etc.
What do we know about ___?	Teacher divides class into two groups and asks them to pool what they know about a certain character in the text, write it down and then groups alternate in revealing what they have come up with. Group with the most correct responses wins. Variation: Group member makes a statement about a character in the text. Other group has to guess whether statement is true or false.
What time is it?	Make clocks out of paper plates with cut-out hands attached with simple brass brad. Teacher playfully asks students to set their clocks at time he orally states. Then he asks students to say what time his clock is set for.
Taxi!	Groups of three. Arrange chairs appropriately. One student is driver, others are passengers. Anecdotes, questions in the new city, life histories, adventures, etc.
Bus tour	Similar to Taxi! More students involved. One is tour guide.
Floor Plan	Teacher suggests possibility of the class winning the lottery and building a group dream house. Students suggest design, furnishings, house rules, etc.
Restaurant	First, similar to "Café", a skit visiting an ethnic restaurant. Finally, an actual class outing to an ethnic restaurant.
Orient Express	Students arrange chairs into European train compartments. They can take on new identities for trip and discover each other's identities in the compartment. New imaginary biographies. Conductor comes: questions, intrigues, etc.
Dream trip	Teacher leads a suggestive fantasy to another country, sets stage, students fill in with imagination and write down their trip. Then read it to each other.

Appendix 3

ACTFL Provisional Proficiency Guidelines

German--Speaking

Novice--Low   Unable to function in spoken German. Oral production is limited to occasional isolated words such as *ja, nein, ich, Sie, Fritz* (name), *Fräulein.* Essentially no communicative ability.

Novice--Mid   Able to operate only in a very limited capacity within very predictable areas of need. Vocabulary is limited to that necessary to express simple elementary needs and basic courtesy formulae such as *Guten Tag / Morgen; Auf Wiedersehen; Das ist . .* (name), *was ist . . .; Wer ist das? Danke; Bitte; Grüß Gott.* Speakers at this level cannot create original sentences or cope with the simplest situations. Pronunciation is frequently unintelligible and is strongly influenced by the first language. Can be understood only with difficulty, even by persons such as teachers who are used to dealing with non-native speakers or in interactions where the context strongly supports the utterance.

Novice--High   Able to satisfy immediate needs using learned utterances. There is no consistent ability to create original sentences or cope with simple survival situations. Can ask questions or make statements with reasonable accuracy only where this involves short memorized utterances or formulae. Vocabulary is limited to common areas such as colors, days of the week, months of the year, names of basic objects, numbers, and names of immediate family members--*Vater, Mutter, Geschwister.* Grammar shows only a few parts of speech. Verbs are generally in the present tense. Errors are frequent and, in spite of repetition, may severely inhibit communication even with persons used to dealing with such learners. Unable to make one's needs known and communicate essential information in a simple survival situation.

Intermediate
--Low

Able to satisfy basic survival needs and minimum courtesy requirements. In areas of immediate need or in very familiar topics, can ask and answer some simple questions and respond to and sometimes initiate simple statements. Can make one's needs known with great difficulty in a simple survival situation, such as ordering a meal, getting a hotel room, and asking for directions; vocabulary is adequate to talk simply about learning the target language and other academic studies. For example: *Wieviel kostet das? Wo ist der Bahnhof? Ich möchte zu .... Wieviel Uhr ist es? Ich lerne hier Deutsch; Ich studiere schon 2 Jahre; Ich habe eine Wohnung.* Awareness of gender apparent (many mistakes). Word order is random. Verbs are generally in the present tense. Some correct use of predicate adjectives and personal pronouns *(ich, wir)* . No clear distinction made between polite and familiar address forms *(Sie, du).* Awareness of case system sketchy. Frequent errors in all structures. Misunderstandings frequently arise from limited vocabulary and grammar and erroneous phonology, but, with repetition, can generally be understood by native speakers in regular contact with foreigners attempting to speak German. Little precision in information conveyed owing to tentative state of grammatical development and little or no use of modifiers.

Intermediate
--Mid

Able to satisfy most routine travel and survival needs and some limited social demands. Can ask and answer questions on very familiar topics and in areas of immediate need. Can initiate and respond to simple statements, and can maintain simple face-to-face conversation. Can ask and answer questions and carry on a conversation on topics beyond basic survival needs or involving the exchange of personal information, i.e., can talk simply about autobiographical information, leisure time activities, academic subjects. Can handle simple transactions at the post office, bank, drugstore, etc. Misunderstandings arise because of limited vocabulary, frequent grammatical errors, and poor pronunciation and intonation, although speakers at this level have broader vocabulary and/or greater grammatical and phonological control than speakers at Intermediate-Low. Speech is often characterized by long pauses. Some grammatical accuracy in some basic structures, i.e., subject-verb agreement, word order in simple statements (excluding adverbs) and interrogative forms, present tense of irregular verbs and imperative of separable prefix verbs *(Kommen Sie mit!).* Fluency is still strained but may be quite natural while within familiar territory. Is generally understood by persons used to dealing with foreigners.

Intermediate Able to satisfy most survival needs and limited social demands.
--High Developing flexibility in language production although fluency is still uneven. Can initiate and sustain a general conversation on factual topics beyond basic survival needs. Can give autobiographical information and discuss leisure time activities. Most verbs are still in the present tense, more common past participles appear (*gegangen, gesehen, geschlafen*). Many mistakes in choice of auxiliary (*habe gegangen* with the present perfect). Past tense is attempted also with common imperfect forms (*sagte, hatte, war*). Several high-frequency separable prefix verbs appear in the indicative (*ich gehe mit*). There is inconsistent coding of proper dative and accusative cases following prepositions in singular and plural. Attempts to expand discourse which is only accurate in short sentences. Frequently gropes for words. Comprehensible to native speakers used to dealing with foreigners, but still has to repeat utterances frequently to be understood by the general public.

Advanced Able to satisfy routine social demands and limited school and work requirements. Can handle with confidence but not with facility most social and general conversations. Can narrate, describe and explain in past, present, and future time. Can communicate facts--what, who, when, where, how much--and can explain a point of view, in an uncomplicated fashion, but cannot conjecture or coherently support an opinion. Can talk in a general way about topics of current public interest (e.g., current events, student rules and regulations), as well as personal interest (work, leisure time activities) and can give autobiographical information. Can make factual comparisons (e.g., life in a city vs. life in a rural area). Can handle work related requirements, needing help in handling any complications or difficulties. Can make a point forcefully and communicate needs and thoughts in a situation with a complication (e.g., calling a mechanic for help with a stalled car, losing traveler's checks). Has a speaking vocabulary sufficient to respond simply with some circumlocutions. Can be understood by native speakers not used to dealing with foreigners, in spite of some pronunciation difficulties. Good control of all verbs in present tense, past participles of most verbs, simple past tense of most irregular verbs, modal auxiliaries, most separable verbs and some reflexives. Double infinitives in main clauses may be attempted (mistakes are expected). Genders of high frequency words are mostly correct. Some inaccuracy in choice of prepositions as well as in distinctions between position and motion. Speaker is hesitant at times and gropes for words, uses paraphrases and fillers, uncomplicated dependent clauses (*daß, weil*) but mistakes are expected when sentences are joined in limited discourse.

Advanced Plus Able to satisfy most school and work requirements and show some ability to communicate on concrete topics relating to particular interests and special fields of competence. Can narrate, describe, and explain in past, present, and future time. Can consistently communicate facts and explain points of view in an uncomplicated fashion. Shows some ability to support opinions, explain in detail, and hypothesize, although only sporadically. Can discuss topics of current and personal interest, and can handle most situations that arise in everyday life (see Advanced Level examples) but will have difficulty with unfamiliar situations (e.g., losing a contact lens in a sink drain and going to a neighbor to borrow a wrench). Normally controls general vocabulary with some groping still evident. Speaking performance is often uneven (e.g., strong in either grammar or vocabulary but not in both). Good control of most verbs in present and past tense and most imperative forms. Irregular control of infinitive clauses with zu, conditional sentences (with *würde* plus infinitive, *hätte, wäre, könnte,* and *da(r)-* and *wo(r)-* compounds). Better control of prepositions and adjective endings but mistakes will occur. Control of dependent clauses. Distinguishes between subordinating and coordinating conjunctions and how they affect word order *(denn, weil).* Good control of limited discourse, but many errors in all more complicated structures. Often shows remarkable fluency and ease of speech, but under tension or pressure language may break down.

Superior Able to speak the language with sufficient structural accuracy and vocabulary to participate in most formal and informal conversations on practical, social, and professional topics. Can discuss particular interests and special fields of competence with reasonable ease. Can support opinions, hypothesize, and conjecture. May not be able to tailor language to fit various audiences or discuss highly abstract topics in depth. Vocabulary is broad enough that speaker rarely has to grope for a word; good use of circumlocution. Pronunciation may still be obviously foreign. Control of grammar is good. Sporadic errors but no patterns of error in tenses, cases, attributive adjectives, pronouns, most verbs plus preposition, dependent clauses, subjunctive II (present and past). Control less consistent in low frequency structures such as passive plus modals, the *lassen* construction, verbs plus specific prepositions *(achten auf, sich halten an, sich irren in),* directional adverbs *(hinauf, hinunter, herüber),* double infinitives in dependent clauses *(daß er das nicht hat machen sollen).* Varying degrees of competence in usage of idiomatic expression and slang. Errors never interfere with understanding and rarely disturb the native speaker.

Appendix 4

Defense Language Institute (DLI) Skill Level Descriptions

SPEAKING

Level 0

Unable to function in the spoken language. Oral production is limited to occasional isolated words. Essentially no communicative ability.

Level 0+

Able to satisfy immediate needs using learned utterances. There is no real autonomy of expression, although there may be some emerging signs of spontaneity and flexibility. There is a slight increase in utterance length but frequent long pauses and repetition of interlocutor's words still occur. Can ask questions or make statements with reasonable accuracy only where this involves short memorized utterances or formulae. Most utterances are telegraphic, and word endings (both inflectional and non-inflectional) are often omitted, confused or distorted. Vocabulary is limited to areas of immediate survival needs. Can differentiate most phonemes when produced in isolation but when they are combined in words or groups of words, errors are frequent and, even with repetition, may severely inhibit communication even with persons used to dealing with such learners. Little development in stress and intonation is evident.

Level 1

Able to satisfy basic survival needs and minimum courtesy requirements. In areas of immediate need or on very familiar topics, can ask and answer simple questions, can ask directions, initiate and respond to simple statements, and maintain very simple face-to-face conversations. (Within the scope of very limited language experience can understand simple questions and statements, allowing for slowed speech, repetition or paraphrase.) When asked to do so, is able to formulate some questions with limited constructions and much inaccuracy. Almost every utterance contains fractured syntax and other grammatical errors. Vocabulary inadequate to express anything but the most elementary needs. Strong interference from the native language occurs in articulation, stress and intonation. Limited vocabulary and grammar and erroneous phonology frequently cause misunderstandings on the part of the interlocutors. With repetition such a speaker can make himself understood to native speakers in regular contact with foreigners. Little precision in information conveyed owing to tentative state of grammatical development and little or no use of modifiers.

Level 1+

Able to satisfy most survival needs and limited social demands. Developing flexibility in a range of circumstances beyond immediate survival needs. Shows spontaneity in language production but fluency is very uneven. Can initiate and sustain a general conversation but has little understanding of the social conventions of conversation. Limited vocabulary range necessitates hesitation and circumlocution. The commoner forms referring to present, past and future occur but errors are frequent in formation and selection. Can use most question forms. While some word order is established errors still occur in more complex patterns. Cannot sustain coherent structures in longer utterances or unfamiliar situations. Ability to describe and give precise information is limited. Aware of basic cohesive features (e.g., pronouns, verb inflection), but many are unreliable, especially if less immediate in reference. Accuracy in elementary constructions is evident although not consistent. Extended discourse is largely a series of short, discrete utterances. Articulation is comprehensible to native speakers used to dealing with foreigners, and can combine most phonemes with reasonable comprehensibility but still has difficulty in producing certain sounds in certain positions, or in certain combinations, and speech will usually be labored. Still has to repeat utterances frequently to be understood by the general public. Able to produce quite consistent narration in either past or future.

Level 2

Able to satisfy routine social demands and limited work requirements. Can handle with confidence but not with facility most social situations including introductions and casual conversations about current events, as well as work, family, and autobiographical information; can handle limited work requirements, needing help in handling any complications or difficulties. (Can get the gist of most conversations on non-technical subjects, i.e., topics which require no specialized knowledge.) Can give directions from one place to another. Has a speaking vocabulary sufficient to respond simply with some circumlocutions; accent, though often quite faulty, is intelligible; can usually handle elementary constructions quite accurately but does not have thorough, confident control of the grammar.

Level 2+

Able to satisfy most work requirements and show some ability to communicate on concrete topics relating to particular interests and special fields of competence. Often shows remarkable fluency and ease of speech but under tension or pressure language may break down. Generally strong in either grammar or vocabulary but not in both. Weaknesses or unevenness in one of the foregoing or in pronunciation result in occasional miscommunication. Areas of weakness range from simple constructions such as plurals, articles, prepositions, and negatives to more complex structures such as tense usage, passive constructions, word order, and relative clauses. Normally controls general vocabulary with some groping for everyday vocabulary still evident.

Level 3

Able to speak the language with sufficient structural accuracy and vocabulary to participate effectively in most formal and informed conversations on practical, social and professional topics. Can discuss particular interests and special fields of competence with reasonable ease. (Comprehension is quite complete for a normal rate of speech.) Vocabulary is broad enough that rarely has to grope for a word, accent may be obviously foreign; control of grammar good, errors virtually never interfere with understanding and rarely disturb the native speaker.

Level 3+

Able to speak the language with sufficient structural accuracy and vocabulary to use it on some levels normally pertinent to professional needs. Shows strength above the base level in one or more but not all of the following: vocabulary, fluency or grammar. May exhibit hesitancy which indicates uncertainty or effort in speech or grammatical errors which limit the level despite obvious strengths in pronunciation, fluency, vocabulary or sociolinguistic cultural factors.

Level

Able to use the language fluently and accurately on all levels normally pertinent to professional needs. Can (understand and) participate in any conversation within the range of own personal and professional experience with a high degree of fluency and precision of vocabulary; would rarely be taken for a native speaker, but can respond appropriately even in unfamiliar situations; errors of pronunciation and grammar quite rare; can handle informal interpreting from and into the language.

Level 4+

Speaking proficiency sometimes equivalent to that of a well-educated native speaker but cannot sustain performance. Weaknesses may be in breadth of vocabulary and idiom, colloquialisms, pronunciation, cultural references or in not responding in a totally native manner.

Level 5

Speaking proficiency equivalent to that of a well-educated native speaker. Has complete fluency in the language such that speech on all levels is fully accepted by educated native speakers in all of its features, including breadth of vocabulary and idiom, colloquialisms and pertinent cultural references.

LISTENING

Level O

No practical understanding of the spoken language. Understanding is limited to occasional isolated words with essentially no ability to comprehend communication.

Level 0+

Sufficient comprehension to understand a number of memorized utterances in areas of immediate needs. Slight increase in utterance length understood but requires frequent long pauses between understood phrases and repeated requests on the listener's part for repetition. Understands with reasonable accuracy only when this involves short memorized utterances or formulae. Utterances understood are relatively short in length. Misunderstandings arise due to ignoring or inaccurately hearing sounds or word endings (both inflectional and non-inflectional), distorting the original meaning. Can understand best those statements where context strongly supports the utterance's meaning. Gets some main ideas.

Level 1

Sufficient comprehension to understand utterances about basic survival needs and minimum courtesy and travel requirements. In areas of immediate need or on very familiar topics, can understand simple questions and answers, simple statements and very simple face-to-face conversations in a standard dialect. These must often be delivered more clearly than normal at a rate slower than normal, with frequent repetitions or paraphrase (that is, by a native used to dealing with foreigners). Once learned, these sentences can be varied for similar level vocabulary and grammar and still be understood. In the majority of utterances, misunderstandings arise due to overlooked or misunderstood syntax and other grammatical clues. Comprehension vocabulary inadequate to understand anything but the most elementary needs. Strong interference from the candidate's native language occurs. Little precision in the information understood owing to tentative state of passive grammar and lack of vocabulary. Comprehension areas include basic needs such as meals, lodging, transportation, time and simple directions (including both route instructions and orders from customs officials, policemen, etc.). Understands main ideas.

Level 1+

Sufficient comprehension to understand short conversations about all survival needs and limited social demands. Developing flexibility evident in understanding into a range of circumstances beyond immediate survival needs. Shows spontaneity in understanding by speed but consistency of understanding uneven. Limited vocabulary range necessitates repetition for understanding. Understands commoner time forms and most question forms, some word order patterns, but miscommunication still occurs with more complex patterns. Cannot sustain understanding of coherent structures in longer utterances or in unfamiliar situations. Understanding of descriptions and the giving of precise information is limited. Aware of basic cohesive features, e.g., pronouns, verb inflections, but many are unreliably understood, especially if less immediate in reference. Understanding is largely limited to a series of short, discrete utterances. Still has to ask for utterances to be repeated. Some ability to understand the facts.

Level 2

Sufficient comprehension to understand conversations on routine social demands and limited job requirements. Able to understand face-to-face speech in a standard dialect, delivered at a normal rate with some repetition and rewording, by a native speaker not used to dealing with foreigners, about everyday topics, common personal and family news, well-known current events, and routine office matters through descriptions and narration about current, past and future events; can follow essential points of discussion or speech at an elementary level on topics in his/her special professional field. Only understands occasional words and phrases of statements made in unfavorable conditions, for example through loudspeakers outdoors. Understands factual content. Interference in understanding caused by native language receding. Able to understand the facts, i.e., the lines but not between or beyond the lines.

Level 2+

Sufficient comprehension to understand most routine social demands and most conversations on work requirements as well as some discussions on concrete topics related to particular interests and special fields of competence. Often shows remarkable ability and ease of understanding, but under tension or pressure may break down. Candidate may display weakness or deficiencies due to inadequate vocabulary base or less than secure knowledge of grammar and syntax. Normally understands general vocabulary with some hesitant understanding of everyday vocabulary still evident. Can sometimes detect emotional overtones. Some ability to understand between the lines (i.e. to grasp inferences).

Level 3

Able to understand the essentials of all speech in a standard dialect including technical discussions within a special field. Has effective understanding of face-to-face speech, delivered with normal clarity and speed in a standard dialect, on general topics and areas of special interest; understands hypothesizing and supported opinions. Has broad enough vocabulary that rarely has to ask for paraphrasing or explanation. Can follow accurately the essentials of conversations between educated native speakers, reasonably clear telephone calls, radio broadcasts, news stories similar to wire service reports, oral reports, some oral technical reports and public addresses on non-technical subjects, can understand without difficulty all forms of standard speech concerning special professional field. Does not understand native speakers if they speak very quickly or use some slang or dialect. Can often detect emotional overtones. Can understand between the lines (i.e., grasp inferences).

Level 3+

Comprehends most of the content and intent of a variety of forms and styles of speech pertinent to professional needs, as well as general topics and social conversation. Ability to comprehend many sociolinguistic and cultural references. However, may miss some subtleties and nuances. Increased ability to comprehend unusually complex structures in lengthy utterances and to comprehend many distinctions in language tailored for different audiences. Increased ability to understand native speakers talking quickly, using nonstandard dialect or slang;

however, comprehension not complete. Emerging ability to understand "beyond the lines" in addition to strong ability to understand "between the lines."

Level 4

Able to understand all forms and styles of speech pertinent to professional needs. Able to understand fully all speech with extensive and precise vocabulary, subtleties and nuances in all standard dialects on any subject relevant to professional needs within the range of his/her experience, including social conversations, all intelligible broadcasts and telephone calls; and many kinds of technical discussions and discourse. Understands language specifically tailored (including persuasion, representation, counseling, and negotiating) to different audiences. Able to understand the essentials of speech in some non-standard dialects. Has difficulty in understanding extreme dialect and slang, also in understanding speech in unfavorable conditions, for example through bad loudspeakers outdoors. Understands "beyond the lines" all forms of the language directed to the general listener, (i.e., able to develop and analyze the argumentation presented).

Level 4+

Increased ability to understand extremely difficult and abstract speech as well as ability to understand all forms and styles of speech pertinent to professional needs, including social conversations. Increased ability to comprehend native speakers using extreme nonstandard dialects and slang as well as to understand speech in unfavorable conditions. Strong sensitivity to sociolinguistic and cultural references. Accuracy is close to that of the educated native listener but still not equivalent.

Level 5

Comprehension equivalent to that of the well-educated native listener. Able to understand fully all forms and styles of speech intelligible to the well-educated native listener, including a number of regional and illiterate dialects, highly colloquial speech and conversations and discourse distorted by marked interference from other noise. Able to understand how natives think as they create discourse. Able to understand extremely difficult and abstract speech.

READING

Level 0

No practical ability to read the language; consistently misunderstands or cannot comprehend at all.

Level 0+

Can recognize all the letters in the printed version of an alphabetic system and high-frequency elements of a syllabary or a character system. Able to read some or all of the following: numbers, isolated words and phrases, personal and place names, street signs, office and shop designations. But not able to read connected prose. Often the above read inaccurately.

Level 1

Sufficient comprehension to read simplest connected written material, authentic or especially prepared for testing, in a form equivalent to usual printing or typescript. Can read either representations of familiar formulaic verbal exchanges or simple language containing only the highest frequency grammatical patterns and vocabulary items (including cognates when appropriate). Able to read and understand previously mastered materials that have been recombined in new ways to achieve different meanings at the same level. Texts may include simple narratives of routine behavior, concrete descriptions of persons, places or things, and explanations of geography and government such as those simplified for tourists. Misunderstandings common. Can get main ideas.

Level 1+

Sufficient comprehension to understand simple discourse for informative social purposes in printed form. Can read material such as announcements of public events, popular advertising notes containing biographical information or narration of events and straightforward newspaper headlines. Can guess at unfamiliar vocabulary if highly contextualized but has difficulty with unfamiliar contexts. Relies primarily on lexical items as time indicators. Has some difficulty with the cohesive factors in discourse, such as matching pronouns with referents. May have to read materials several times for understanding.

Level 2

Sufficient comprehension to read simple authentic written material in a form equivalent to usual printing or typescript on subjects within a familiar context. Can read uncomplicated but authentic prose on familiar subjects that are normally presented in a predictable sequence, which aids the reader in understanding. Texts may include description and narration in contexts such as news items describing frequently occurring events, simple biographical information, social notices, formatted business letters and simple technical material written for the general reader. The prose is predominantly in familiar sentence patterns. Can follow essential points of written discussion at an elementary level on topics in his/her special professional field. Some misunderstandings. Able to read the facts, i.e., the lines but not between or beyond the lines.

Level 2+

Sufficient comprehension to understand most factual material in non-technical prose as well as some discussions on concrete topics related to special professional interests. Reading ability still dependent on subject matter knowledge. Can locate and interpret the main ideas and details in material written for the general reader. Is able to separate the main ideas from lesser ones and uses that distinction to advance understanding. Has begun to make sensible guesses about unfamiliar words by using linguistic context and prior knowledge. May react personally to material but does not yet detect subjective attitudes, values or judgements in the writing.

Level 3

Able to read with almost complete comprehension at normal speed authentic prose on unfamiliar subjects. Reading ability is not dependent on subject matter knowledge. Texts will include news stories similar to wire service reports, routine correspondence, general reports and technical material in his/her professional field, all of which include hypothesis, argumentation and supported opinions. Such texts typically include grammatical patterns and vocabulary ordinarily encountered in professional reading. Misreading rare. Almost always able to correctly interpret material, relate ideas and make inferences. Rarely has to pause over or reread general vocabulary. However, may experience some difficulty with unusually complex structure and low frequency idioms.

Level 3+

Increased ability to comprehend a variety of styles and forms of language pertinent to professional needs. Rarely misinterprets such texts or rarely experiences difficulty relating ideas or making inferences. Ability to comprehend many sociolinguistic and cultural references. However, may miss some nuances and subtleties. Increased ability to comprehend unusually complex structures and low frequency idioms; however, accuracy is not complete.

Level 4

Able to read fluently and accurately all styles and forms of the language pertinent to professional needs. Can read more difficult prose and follow unpredictable turns of thought readily in any area directed to the general reader and all materials in his/her own special field including official and professional documents and correspondence. Able to read and understand precise and extensive vocabulary including nuances and subtleties and recognize all professionally relevant vocabulary known to the educated non-professional native, although may have some difficulty with slang. Can read reasonably legible handwriting without difficulty. Understands almost all sociolinguistic and cultural references. Accuracy nearly that of an educated native reader. Able to read beyond the lines.

Level 4+

Increased ability to read extremely difficult or abstract prose. Increased ability to read and understand a variety of vocabulary, idioms, colloquialisms and slang. Strong sensitivity to sociolinguistic and cultural references. Increased ability to read less than fully legible handwriting. Increased ability to read beyond the lines. Accuracy is close to that of the educated native reader but still not equivalent.

Level 5

Reading proficiency equivalent to that of well-educated native reader. Can read extremely difficult and abstract prose, e.g., legal, technical as well as highly colloquial writings and the literary forms of the language. Reads and understands a wide variety of vocabulary and idiom, colloquialisms, slang and pertinent cultural references. With varying degrees of difficulty can read all kinds of handwritten documents. Able to understand how natives think as they produce a text. Accuracy is equivalent to that of a well-educated native reader.

References

Forward

1 The best source of information and research results in the field of accelerated learning, suggestopedia, and related holistic models is the Journal of the Society for Accelerative Learning and Teaching (SALT), 1976 - current. The journal is accessible through ERIC or may be ordered from the Society for Accelerated Learning and Teaching, Box 1216, Welch Station, Ames, Iowa 50011. Among the books on the subject I would recommend are those by Jensen, Kline, Lawlor, Lozanov, Merritt, Quina, and Schuster, the full references for which can be found in the Bibliography.

2 Assagioli's main works are *Psychosynthesis* and *The Act of Will*. Another excellent book on Psychosynthesis is P. Ferrucci's *What We May Be*. See full Bibliography for exact references.
A good introduction to Jung's work is his *Man and His Symbols*. Garden City, N.Y.: Doubleday, 1964.

3 Lozanov, Georgi. *Suggestology and the Outlines of Suggestopedy*. New York: Gordon and Breach, 1979.
Lozanov, G. "Suggestology and Suggestopedia, Theory and Practice." *UNESCO Report*, ED-78/WS/119, 1978.
Lozanov, Georgi. *Foreign Language Teacher's Manual*. News York: Gordon & Breach, 1988.

4 Krashen, Stephen. *Principles and Practice in Second Language Acquisition*. New York: Pergamon Press, 1982.

5 Asher, James J. *Learning Another Language Through Actions*. Third Edition. Los Gatos, California: Sky Oaks Productions, 1986.

6 Krashen, Stephen and Terrell, Tracy. *The Natural Approach*. San Francisco: Alemany Press, 1983.

Chapter 1

7 One of the most constructive examples of such criticism which goes on to offer specific corrective strategies is Betty Edwards. Her *Drawing on the Right Side of the Brain* is an excellent manual for the art of drawing as well as good background in brain theory. Similarly, Gabriele Lusser-Rico's *Writing Naturally* provides a highly useful model for writing, using contemporary brain theories.

8 R. Ornstein, *The Psychology of Consciousness* (New York: Harcourt, Brace, Jovanovich, 1977).

9   H. Gardner, "What We Know (and Don't Know) about the Two Halves of the Brain," *Harvard Magazine* 80 (1978): 24-27.

10*UNESCO Report*, p. 25.

11S. Springer and G. Deutsch, *Left Brain, Right Brain*. Third Edition. New York: Freeman and Co., 1989, p. 298.

12Springer and Deutsch, 1989, p. 287.

13Springer and Deutsch, 1989, p. 286.

14New York: Random House, 1977.

15*Human Brain and Human Learning*. New York: Longman, 1983. See also *How the Brain Works*. New York: Basic Books, 1975.

16*UNESCO Report*, p. 24.

17Hart, 1983, p. 52. Stress mine.

18Hart, 1983, p. 55. Stress mine.

19*UNESCO Report*, p. 25.

20Hart, 1983, p. 57. Stress mine.

21Hart, 1983, p. 60.

22Hart, 1983, p. 60. Stress mine.

23Hart, 1983, p. 162f.

24Hart, 1983, p. 164.

25Hart, 1983, p. 164.

26Hart, 1983, p. 164.

27Such as Asher, Krashen, Terrell and Lozanov.

28Hart, 1983, p. 164. Stress mine.

29Hart, 1983, p. 164.

30Hart, 1983, p. 164.

31Hart, 1983, p. 108

32Hart, 1983, p. 109.

33Hart, 1983, p. 109

Chapter 2

34A good first introduction to Lozanov's work is the report he prepared for the UNESCO team which visited his research center in 1978. See Lozanov, Georgi. "Suggestology and Suggestopedia, Theory and Practice," *UNESCO Report*, ED-78/WS/119, 1978.
Lozanov's major work is *Suggestology and the Outlines of Suggestopedy*, New York: Gordon and Breach, 1979. It is heavy reading, filled with the jargon of East European social science research, but there are many pearls to be found. It is a must for an indepth understanding of Lozanov.

The Journal of the Society for Accelerative-Learning and Teaching is a good source of articles on Lozanov and his ideas. See Bibliography.

[35]*UNESCO Report*, p. 1.

[36]*UNESCO Report*, p. 31.

[37]Lozanov: *Suggestology* ...., p. 201.

[38]Lozanov: *Suggestology* ...., p. 201.

[39]Lozanov: *UNESCO Report*, p. 14.

[40]Lozanov: *UNESCO Report*, p. 15.

[41]Neuro-Linguistic Programming (NLP), which has valuable applications for teaching and learning, is presented in numerous books. See the titles in the Bibliography under Bandler, Grinder, Gordon and Lankton.

[42]*UNESCO Report*, p. 18.

[43]Lozanov: *Suggestology* ...., p. 97f.

[44]*UNESCO Report*, p. 32f.

[45]*UNESCO Report*, p. 33.

[46]*UNESCO Report*, p. 33.

[47]*UNESCO Report*, p. 35.

[48]*UNESCO Report*, p. 36.

[49]*UNESCO Report*, p. 37.

[50]*UNESCO Report*, p. 38.

Chapter 3

[51]The reporting of Lozanov's research results and data from his foreign language programs can be found in his *Suggestology. . .* 1979. See Bibliography.

[52]See titles in Bibliography under Bancroft, Benitez-Bordon, Bushman, Caskey, Miele, Ostrander, Prichard, and Schuster.

[53]The Society for Accelerative Learning and Teaching (SALT) holds an annual international conference which brings together teachers and researchers from a wide range of subject areas to report research results and exchange ideas in the field of accelerative approaches to learning and teaching. Although foreign language pedagogy occupies only one focus among many in SALT, some of the pioneering FL applications in America of Lozanov's work have been reported there.

[54]Krashen, 1982, P. 10.

[55]Krashen and Terrell, *The NaturalApproach,* 1983, p. 26.

[56]Lozanov, *Suggestology. . . .* 1979, pp.12-32. Here Lozanov reports the results of his FL program.

[57]Krashen and Terrell, *The Natural Approach*, 1983, p. 27

[58]Krashen and Terrell, *The Natural Approach*, 1983, p. 28

[59]This point is made in conjunction with his fourth hypothesis, the "Input hypothesis".

[60]Krashen and Terrell, *The Natural Approach*, 1983, p. 30

[61]Ibid.

[62]Krashen and Terrell, *The Natural Approach*, 1983, p. 30

[63]Krashen, 1982, p. 19.

[64]Krashen, 1982, p. 19f.

[65]Krashen and Terrell, *The Natural Approach*, 1983, p. 32

[66]Krashen and Terrell, *The Natural Approach*, 1983, p. 33

[67]Krashen and Terrell, *The Natural Approach*, 1983, p. 35

[68]Krashen and Terrell, *The Natural Approach*, 1983, p. 35

[69]Krashen and Terrell, *The Natural Approach*, 1983, p. 38

[70]Krashen and Terrell, *The Natural Approach*, 1983, p. 38

[71]Krashen and Terrell, *The Natural Approach*, 1983, p. 38

[72]Krashen and Terrell, *The Natural Approach*, 1983, p. 39f.

[73]Asher, James, *Learning Another Language Through Actions: The Complete Teacher's Guidebook.* Expanded Third Edition. Los Gatos, CA: Sky Oaks Productions, 1986.

[74]Asher, 1986, p. 2-17f.

[75]Asher, 1986, p. 2-25.

[76]Asher, 1986, p. 2-4.

[77]See titles in Bibliography under Segal, Seely, and Francois.

[78]This and the following discussion are adapted from written statements in printed but unpublished materials and oral statements, all from a workshop on the Natural Approach given by Terrell for the Massachusetts Foreign Language Association, November 8, 1986).

[79]Ibid

[80]Ibid

[81]Ibid

Chapter 4

[82]See titles in Bibliography under Lozanov, Krashen, Terrell, Asher and Madsen.

[83] Hart, 1983, p. 96.

[84] Hart, 1983, p. 98f.

[85]Full-spectrum fluorescent lights contain the light-wave properties of normal, natural light. Regular fluorescent lighting contains only a portion of the natural light spectrum, commonly resulting in fatigue, headaches, depressed energy, etc. Full-spectrum bulbs are readily available in larger supply firms of lighting products. Health food stores also frequently carry them.

[86]An excellent discussion of colors as well as of environmental factors in general is the book by Carol Venolia, *Healing Environments.* Berkeley, California: Celestial Arts, 1989. Venolia writes:

Green is a mixture of blue (spirituality and calm) and yellow (wisdom). . . Sometimes called "the master healer," green affects the whole system and is especially beneficial to the central nervous system. . . Green subdues nervousness and tension and is good for concentration and meditation. It soothes emotional disorders and nervous headaches.

Yellow vitalizes and accelerates mental activity and feelings of joy. . . Yellow can relieve depression, tension, and fear, and soothe mental and nervous exhaustion . . . As a mental, creative color, yellow is good to use in libraries, study areas, or any place where mental pursuits will be undertaken.

Blue lowers blood pressure, pulse rate, heartbeat, muscle activity, eyeblinds, and brain waves. The effect is restful and sedating, bestowing quietude, gentleness, contentment and composure. . . Blue counteracts impulsiveness, violence, and restlessness. . . Blue in the environment has been found to reduce hyperactivity in schoolchildren significantly, but it would be a poor choice for a social area since it may suppress conversation.

Orange is the combination of yellow (wisdom) and red (physicality, action, and power), and therefore is seen as more disciplined and practical than red. It symbolizes optimism, courage, enthusiasm, and confidence. . . A social color, it is well used in community centers, meeting places, family rooms. . . As the color of ideas, orange is also good to use in areas for creative study. . . Touches of orange in the environment can counteract depression and humorlessness. (The preceding passages are taken from pages 64-66 of Venolia's book)

[87]See Rosenthal, R. and Jacobson, L. *Pygmalion in the Classroom,* New York: Holt, Rinehart & Winston, 1968. Also: Rosenthal, R. "The Pygmalion Effect Lives", *Psychology Today* 7:4, pp. 56-63.

[88]Excellent resources for centering as well as visualization techniques are the books by Bry, DeMille, Hendricks and Houston, listed in the Bibliography.

Chapter 5

[89]"Cultural Microrhythms," in *Interaction Rhythms*, 1982, pp. 53-77.

[90]"Language Learning and Communication," *The French Review*, Vol. LVIII, No. 6, May 1985, pp. 777-785.

[91]Fidelman is author and project director of a multi-year grant from FIPSE entitled *In the French Body*.

[92]The disk was part of a language learning project developed by Wylie and Fidelman. The project utilizes computer-assisted videodisc technology together with a holistic approach to the communication process to help students learn to use their bodies as an integral part of learning to communicate in French. Wylie writes: "We communicate with every means at our disposal, so the whole body, not just the parts that produce speech, must be trained to communicate in a foreign language." (Wylie, op.cit., p. 778. for more information on Fidelman's project and materials, write Carolyn Fidelman, 91 Baldwin Street, Charlestown, MA 02129.

[93]Condon, op.cit., p. 56.

[94]Wylie, op.cit., p. 781.

[95]Ibid

Chapter 6

[96]See titles in Bibliography under Erickson, Bandler, Grinder, Gordon, and Lankton.

[97]For a thorough discussion of representational systems see Bandler, R. and Grinder, J. *Structure of Magic I* and *II*, Palo Alto, California: Science and Behavior Books, 1975 (Vol. I) and 1976 (Vol. II).

[98]Ibid

[99]Taken from workshop materials furnished by Inword Ways, P.O. Box 4596, Berkeley, CA 94704.

[100]A good introduction to Jung's ideas on symbols is his last work, *Man and His Symbols*, Garden City, N.Y.: Doubleday, 1964. For the NLP conception of representational systems, the books by Gordon and Lankton are both clear and concise. (See Bibliography.)

[101]See titles in Bibliography by Bry and DeMille.

[102]David Gordon, *Therapeutic Metaphors.* Cupertino, California: Meta Publications,1978.

[103]See titles in Bibliography by Bandler, Gordon, Grinder, and Lankton.

[104]Lankton, Stephen, *Practical Magic,* 1980, p. 55.

Chapter 7

[105]Lozanov, Georgi, *Suggestology.....* ,1979, p. 97f.

[106]Reported in a paper delivered at the SALT Conference at Ames, Iowa, August, 1983.

[107]See the discussion of Asher in Chapter 3.

[108]Krashen, 1982, p. 60.

[109]Krashen, 1982, p. 74.

[110]Asher, 1986, p. 3-7.

[111]Krashen, 1982, p. 74.

[112]Brown, Roger "Introduction." In. C. Snow and C. Ferguson (Eds.) *Talking to Children.* New York: Cambridge University Press, p. 26. Cited in Krashen (1982), p. 65.

[113]Krashen and Terrell, *The Natural Approach,* p. 28.

[114]Ibid

Chapter 8

[115]These early materials are modeled on those developed by Terrell for the Natural Approach. See especially pp. 95-129 of *The Natural Approach,* by Krashen and Terrell, 1983.

[116]These have varied widely over the years from the traditional *Deutsche Sprache und Landeskunde* by Crean, Scott, Hill and Briggs to the radically communication oriented *Deutsch Natürlich* to Terrell's *Kontakte,* based on the Natural Approach, and to, most recently, *Alles Gute* by Briggs and Crean. I have come to favor a more succinct, traditional text for the course supplement over the more communication-oriented texts, since it is indeed a supplement to my own extensive communication-oriented materials.

Chapter 9

[117]For guided relaxations I prefer certain socalled "New Age" music, because it has less definable meter and structure, has very long, relaxing phrases and lends itself to letting go of boundaries. My favorites are *Spectrum Suite* by Steven Halpern and the tapes of Daniel Kobialka, especially *Dream Passage.*

[118]Krashen and Terrell, *The Natural Approach,* 1983, p. 82.

[119]Krashen, 1982, p. 66.

[120]Some of the earlier variants of Lozanov's method still used by some in the U.S.A., include physical relaxation exercises, yoga breathing, and synchronized breathing together with different intonational

presentations of material. Such variants are described in the SALT manual and the book *Superlearning* by Ostrander and Schroeder (see Bibliography). Lozanov eventually favored a musical presentation: "We dropped artificial intonation later on in our suggestopedic courses and retained only the artistic intonation in harmony with the music of the concert session. In this way, the intonation became more acceptable to the students." (Lozanov, *Suggestology*......., 1979, p. 195f).

[121]Lozanov, *Suggestology*......., 1979, p. 266ff.

[122]Lozanov does not specify slow movements for this concert. He uses the entire baroque piece with movements in all tempi. In my own experience, the slow movements seem to sustain the relaxed atmosphere better.

[123]Lozanov made this assertion in a lecture during his teacher training seminars in Orinda, California in May, 1979.

Chapter 10

[124]A statement made by Ms. Gateva during the instructor training program led by Dr. Lozanov in Orinda, California, May, 1979.

[125]See Krashen and Terrell, *The Natural Approach,* 1983.

Chapter 11

[126]See the discussion of Hart's *Human Brain, Human Learning* in Chapter3.

[127]See Chapter 3 for a discussion of Krashen's theories. See all the Krashen titles in the Bibliography.

[128] Krashen and Terrell, *The Natural Approach,* 1983, p. 71f.

[129]Lozanov, *Suggestology*.... 1979, pp. 96-100.

Chapter 12

[130]The following studies report results using Suggestopedia or close variants under varying levels of controlled conditions:

Benitez-Bordon, R. and D. Schuster. "Foreign Language Learning via the Lozanov Method: Pilot Studies." *Journal of S.A.L.T.,* Vol. 1, No. 1 (Spring 1976).

Benitez-Bordon, R. "The Effects of Suggestive Learning Climate, Synchronized Breathing and Music on the Learning and Retention of Spanish Words." *Journal of S.A.L.T.,* Vol. 1, No. 1 (Spring 1976).

Bushman, R. and Madsen, H. "A Description and Evaluation of Suggestopedia--A New Teaching Methodology." In J. Fanselow and R. Crymes (Eds.) *On TESOL '76*. Washington: TESOL pp. 29-38.

Philipov, E. "Suggestology: The Use of Suggestion in Learning and Hypermnesia." Unpublished dissertation, U.S. International University, San Diego, 1975. Ann Arbor, Mich., University Microfilm 75-20255.

Schuster, D. "A Preliminary Evaluation of the Suggestive-Accelerative Lozanov Method in Teaching Beginning Spanish." *Journal of S.A.L.T.*, Vol. 1, No. 1 (Spring 1976).

The following studies report results of other acquisition approaches:

Asher, J. "The Strategy of Total Physical Response: An Application To Learning Russian." *International Review of Applied Linguistics* 3: 292-9.

Asher, J. "The Total Physical Response Approach to Second Language Learning." *Modern Language Journal* 53: 3-18.

Asher, J and J. Kusudo and R. de la Torre. "Learning a Second Language Through Commands: The Second Field Test." *Modern Language Journal* 58 (no. 102): 24-32.

Terrell, T. "A Natural Approach to the Acquisition and Learning of a Language." *Modern Language Journal* 61: 325-36.

Terrell, T. "The Natural Approach to Language Teaching: An Update." *Modern Language Journal* 66: 121-131.

[131]These have varied widely over the years from the traditional *Deutsche Sprache und Landeskunde* by Crean, Scott, Hill and Briggs to the radically communication oriented *Deutsch Natürlich* to Terrell's *Kontakte*, based on the Natural Approach, and to, most recently, *Alles Gute* by Briggs and Crean. I have come to favor a more succinct, traditional text for the course supplement over the more communication-oriented texts, since it is indeed a supplement to my own extensive commnication-oriented materials.

[132]From a fact sheet on the OPI, obtainable from ACTFL, 6 Executive Boulevard, Upper Level, Yonkers, NY 10701. Tel. (914) 963-8830.

[133]ACTFL Proficiency Guidelines, Generic Descriptions, 1986. Available from ACTFL, 6 Executive Boulevard, Upper Level, Yonkers, NY 10701. Tel. (914) 963-8830.

[134]Write ACTFL at address in previous footnote.

[135]See Appendix 3 for a description of the ACTFL OPI rating scale for German speaking proficiency.

[136]See Chapter 3 for a discussion of the "monitor".

[137]College Level Equivalency Program--under the direction of the Educational Testing Service (ETS).

[138]See Appendix 3 for descriptions of the various competence levels.

[139]"ACTFL Provisional Proficiency Guidelines" published by ACTFL, 6 Executive Boulevard, Upper Level, Yonkers, NY 10701.

[140]See Appendix 3 for a full description of the proficiency levels.

[141]Krashen, Stephen D. *Principles and Practice in Second Language Acquisition,* 1982, p. 33.

Chapter 13

[142]DLI = Defense Language Institute; FSI = Foreign Service Institute. These rating measures are standard for measuring language proficiency throughout U.S. Government agencies. See Appendix 4 for a description of the DLI rating scale. The DLI/FSI standards provided the basis for the development of the ACTFL proficiency guidelines discussed in the previous chapter and described in Appendix 3.

[143]Ibid

[144]See Chapter 3 for a discussion of Krashen's theories. See also the Krashen titles in the Bibliography.

[145]See Chapter 6 for a discussion of the "anchoring" concept.

[146]See Chapter 3 for a discussion of Total Physical Response (TPR).

[147]Ibid

[148]See Chapter 9 for a discussion of the use of music in the ACT Approach.

[149]The use of metaphor, guided fantasy and the metaphorical story is discussed in Chapter 6.

[150]See chapter 10 for a discussion of primary activation techniques.

[151]The "Concert Presentations" I and II are discussed in Chapter 9.

[152]This and several other related techniques are well described in Krashen and Terrell, *The Natural Approach,* 1983, as well in Chapter 3 of this book.

[153]See Chapter 3 for a discussion of the role of "comprehensible input".

[154]See Chapter 3 for a discussion of the role of "comprehensible input".

Chapter 14

[155]Houston, J. 1982. *The Possible Human*. Los Angeles: Tarcher, p. 62.

[156]Krashen and Terrell, *The Natural Approach*, 1983, p. 165.

[157]Ibid, 168-174.

[158]See Gardner, H. 1983. *Frames of Mind. The Theory of Multiple Intelligences*, New York: Basic Books.

Bibliography

Suggestion and Education

Balevski, P. 1975. "EEG changes in the Process of Memorization under Ordinary and Suggestive Conditions." *Suggestology and Suggestopedia* 1:1 pp. 26-36.

Balevski, P. and Ganovski, L. 1975. "The Effect of Some of the Means of Suggestion on the Short-term and Long-term Memory of Students from 11-17 Years." *Suggestology and Suggestopedia* No. 3, pp. 47-52.

Balevski, P. and Ganovski, L. 1975. "The Volume of Short-term Memory at the Beginning of the Course and the Proficiency of Students Learning Foreign Languages by the Suggestopedic System." *Suggestology and Suggestopedia* 2, pp. 22-28.

Bancroft, W.J. 1976. "Suggestology and Suggestopedia: The Theory of the Lozanov Method." *Journal of Suggestive-Accelerative Learning and Teaching* 1:3, pp. 187-216.

Bancroft, W.J. 1975. "The Lozanov Language Class." *Canadian Modern Language Review* 31:2, pp. 3-31.

Bancroft, W. J. 1972. "Foreign Language Teaching in Bulgaria." *Canadian Modern Language Review* 28:2, pp. 9-13.

Benitez-Bordon, R. and Schuster, D. 1976. "Foreign Language Learning via the Lozanov Method: Pilot Studies." *Journal of the Society for Accelerative Learning and Teaching,* 1:1 (Spring 1976).

Benitez-Bordon, R. 1976. "The Effects of Suggestive Learning Climate, Synchronized Breathing and Music on the Learning and Retention of Spanish Words." *Journal of the Society for Accelerative Learning and Teaching,* 1:1.

Baur, R. S. 1990. *Superlearning und Suggestopädie.* Berlin/München: Langenscheidt Verlag.

Bochow,, P., Wagner and Hardy 1988. *Suggestopädie.* Speyer: Gabal.

Bolhöfer, N. 1986. "Suggestopädie : eine Gefahr?" *Neues Lernen Journal,* 2/1986. Bremen: PLS Verlag.

Bröhm-Offenmann, B. 1989. *Suggestopädie. Sanftes Lernen in der Schule.* Göttingen: Verlag Die Werkstatt.

Bushman, R. and Madsen, H. 1976. "A Description and Evaluation of Suggestopedia--A New Teaching Methodology." In J. Fanselow and R. Crymes (Eds.) *On TESOL '76*. Washington: TESOL pp. 29-38.

Caskey, O. and Flake, M. 1976. *Suggestive-Accelerative Learning: Adaptation of the Lozanov Method*, Texas Tech. University.

Clark, B. 1986. Optimizing Learning. The Integrative Education Model in the Classroom. Columbus, Ohio: Merrill Publishing.

Fuerst, K. 1976. "Some Observations of Behavior in a Suggestopedic French Language Class." Journal of Suggestive-Accelerative Learning and Teaching 1:3, pp. 182-186.

Grassi, J. 1984. The Accelerated Learning Process in Science: A Handbook for Teachers. ALPS Products, 369 Singletary Lane, Framingham, MA 01701.

Grassi, J. 1984. Introduction to Geometry: A Curriculum Guide for Elementary Teachers. ALPS Products, 369 Singletary Lane, Framingham, MA 01701.

Gritton, C. 1976. "Practical Issues in Adapting Suggestopedia to an American Classroom" Journal of the Society for Accelerative-Learning and Teaching 1:4.

Gritton, C. and Benitez-Bordon, R. 1976. "Americanizing Suggestopedia: A Preliminary Trial in a U.S.Classroom" Journal of the Society for Accelerative-Learning and Teaching 1:2.

Hinkelmann, G. and Ferreboeuf, M. 1988. *Leichter Lehren*. Bremen: PLS Verlag.

Hinkelmann, K. G. 1986. *Superlearning und Suggestopädie*. Bremen: PLS Verlag.

Holistic Education Review. P.O. Box 1476, Greenfield, MA 01302.

Jensen, E. 1988. *Superteaching*, Turning Point: P.O. Box 2551, Del Mar, CA 92014.

Journal of the Society for Suggestive-Accelerative Learning and Teaching, P.O.Box 1216, Welch Station, Ames, Iowa 50010. 1976-current.

Kline, P. 1976. "The Sandy Spring Experiment: Applying Relaxation Techniques to Learning." *Journal of Suggestive-Accelerative Learning and Teaching* 1:1, pp. 16-26.

Kline, P. 1989. *The Everyday Genius*. Arlngton, Virginia: Great Ocean Publishing.

Lawlor, M. *Inner Track Learning*. Inner Track Learning, Forge House, Kemble, Cirencester, Glos. GL76AD, United Kingdom.

Limbic Plus, The: Jenzen Kelly Associates, Inc., 32260-88th Ave., Lawton, MI 49065-9302.

Lozanov, Georgi. 1988. *Foreign Language Teacher's Manual.* New York: Gordon and Breach Publishing.

Lozanov, G. 1979. *Suggestology and Outlines of Suggestopedia,* New York: Gordon and Breach Publishing.

Lozanov, G. 1978. *Suggestology and Suggestopedia, Theory and Practice,* UNESCO Report ED- 78/WS/119.

Lozanov, G. and Balevski, P. 1975. "The Effect of the Suggestopedic System of Instruction on the Physical Development, State of Health, and Working Capacity of First and Second Grade Pupils." *Suggestology and Suggestopedia* 1:3.

Lozanov, G. 1975. "Suggestopedia in Primary Schools". *Suggestology and Suggestopedia* 1:3.

Lozanov, G. 1975. "The Suggestological Theory of Communication and Instruction." *Suggestology and Suggestopedia* 1:3.

Lozanov, G. 1975. "The Nature and History of the Suggestopedic System of Teaching Foreign Languages and its Experimental Prospects." *Suggestology and Suggestopedia Journal,* 1:1.

Merritt, S. 1987. *Successful, Non-Stressful Learning.* Merritt Learning Systems, San Diego, California, 92103.

Miele, Philip, 1982. *Suggestopedia: The Natural Way to Learn,* Utopia Unlimited Publishing Co., Silver Spring, MD.

Miele, Philip. 1978. "The Power of Suggestion: A New Way of Learning Languages." *Parade Magazine,* March 12.

Noyes, I. 1988. *How to Increase Your Learning Power (A Study-Skills Program),* Educational Skills Center, Inc., 711 West Main, Morristown, TN 37814.

On the Beam (periodical): New Horizons in Learning, 4649 Sunnyside N., Seattle, WA 98103.

Ostrander, Sheila and Schroeder, Lynn. 1979. *Superlearning,* New York: Delacorte Press.

Philipov, E. 1975. "Suggestology: The Use of Suggestion in Learning and Hypermnesia." Unpublished dissertation, U.S. International University, San Diego. Ann Arbor, Mich., University Microfilm 75-20255.

Pollack, C. 1976. "Educational Experiment: Therapeutic Pedagogy." *Journal of the Society for Accelerative-Learning and Teaching* 1:2.

Prichard, A. and Taylor, J. 1980. *Accelerating Learning: The Use of Suggestion in the Classroom,* Academic Therapy Publications, 20 Commercial Boulevard, Novato, CA 94947.

Prichard, A. 1976. "Suggestopedia, A Transpersonal Approach to Learning." *Journal of the Society for Accelerative-Learning and Teaching* 1:3.

Prichard, Allyn. 1976. "Lozanov-Type Suggestion Techniques for Remedial Reading." *Journal of the Society for Accelerative-Learning and Teaching* 1:4.

Quina, J. 1987. *Effective Secondary Teaching: Going Beyond the Bell Curve.* New York: Harper and Row.

Racle, G. 1976. "The Key Principles of Suggestopedia." *Journal of Suggestive-Accelerative Learning and Teaching* 1:3, pp. 149-163.

Racle, G. 1975. "A Suggestopedic Experiment in Canada." *Suggestology and Suggestopedia* 1:1, pp. 45-51.

Rose, C. 1986. *Accelerated Learning.* New York: Dell

Rosenthal, R. and Jacobson, L. 1968. *Pygmalion in the Classroom.* New York: Holt, Rinehart and Winston.

Rosenthal, R. 1975. "The Pygmalion Effect Lives," *Psychology Today* 7:4, pp. 56-63.

Schiffler, L. 1989. *Suggestopädie und Superlearning – empirisch geprüft.* Frankfurt am Main: Diessterweg.

Schuster, D. 1985. *Suggestive Accelerative Learning and Teaching,* New York: Gordon & Breach Publishing.

Schuster, D. 1976. "Introduction to the Lozanov Method," *Journal of the Society for Accelerative-Learning and Teaching* 1:4.

Schuster, D. 1976. "The Effects of the Alpha Mental State, Indirect Suggestion, and Associative Mental Activity on Learning Rare English Words." *Journal of Suggestive-Accelerative Learning and Teaching* 1:2, pp. 116-123.

Schuster, D. 1976. "A Preliminary Evaluation of the Suggestive-Accelerative Lozanov Method in Teaching Beginning Spanish." *Journal of the Society for Accelerative Learning and Teaching,* 1:1.

Society for Accelerative Learning and Teaching / International Resources 1989. SALT, P.O.Box 1216, Welch Station, Ames, Iowa 50010.

Venola, Carol: 1988. *Healing Environments*. Berkeley, CA: Celestial Arts.

Wood, L. 1988. *Chemistry Curriculum Guide*. Leo Wood, 1897 E. Sesame Street, Tempe, Arizona.

Wood, L. 1988. *Lab and Study guide for Chemistry*. Leo Wood, 1897 E. Sesame Street, Tempe, Arizona.

The Brain

Asher, J. 1988. *Brainswitching: A Skill for the 21st Century*. Los Gatos, California: Sky Oaks Productions.

Brain/Mind Bulletin, P.O. Box 42211, Los Angeles, CA 90042.

Buzan, T. 1974. *Use Both Sides of Your Brain*, Dutton.

Chall, J. and Mirsky, A. (editors) 1978. *Education and the Brain. The 77th Yearbook of the National Society for the Study of Education*, Chicago: University of Chicago Press.

Edwards, B. 1979. *Drawing on the Right Side of the Brain*, Tarcher Press.

Ferguson, M. 1977. "Current Brain Research and Human Potential for Learning," *Journal of Suggestive-Acccelerative Learning and Teaching*, 1:4.

Ferguson, M. 1975. *The Brain Revolution*. New York: Bantam.

Gardner, H. 1983. *Frames of Mind. The Theory of Multiple Intelligences*, New York: Basic Books.

Gardner, H. 1978. "What We Know (and Don't Know) about the Two Halves of the Brain," *Harvard Magazine* 80, pp. 24-27.

Hart, L. 1983. *Human Brain and Human Learning*, New York: Longman.

Hart, Leslie. 1975. *How the Brain Works*, Basic Books, New York.

Mac Lean, P. 1978. "A Mind of Three Minds: Educating the Triune Brain," in Chall, J. and Mirsky, A. (editors). *Education and the Brain. The 77th Yearbook of the National Society for the Study of Education*, Chicago: University of Chicago Press.

Restak, R. 1979. *The Brain: The Last Frontier*, Garden City, N.Y. : Doubleday.

Russell, P. 1983. *The Global Brain*, Los Angeles: Tarcher.

Russell, Peter. 1979. *The Brain Book,* Hawthorne Books.

Sagan, Carl. 1977. *The Dragons of Eden,* New York: Random House.

Samples, R.E. 1975. "Learning with the Whole Brain," *Human Behavior* 4, pp. 16-23.

Sperry, R.W. 1966. "Brain Bisection and Consciousness," in *Brain and Conscious Experience,* ed. J. Eccles, New York: Springer-Verlag.

Springer, S. and Deutsch, G. 1989. *Left Brain, Right Brain.* Third Edition. New York: Freeman and Co.

Wittrock, M.C. (ed.) 1980. *The Brain and Psychology.* New York: Academic Press.

Foreign Language Pedagogy

Asher, James J. 1988. *Learning Another Language Through Actions.* Expanded Third Edition. Los Gatos, California: Sky Oaks Productions.

Asher, J. "The Strategy of Total Physical Response: An Application To Learning Russian." *International Review of Applied Linguistics* 3: pp. 292-9.

Asher, J. "The Total Physical Response Approach to Second Language Learning." *Modern Language Journal* 53, pp. 3-18.

Asher, J. and Kusudo, J. and de la Torre, R. "Learning a Second Language Through Commands: The Second Field Test." *Modern Language Journal* 58:102, pp. 24-32.

Curran, C. 1976. *Counseling-Learning in Second Languages.* Apple River, Wisconsin: Apple River Press.

Davalos, D. 1984. *Activities to Expand Learning.* (Written expecially for suggesto-pedia-related, acquisition oriented methods.) 125 West 2nd Ave., Denver, Colorado 80223.

Dulay, H., Burt, M., and Krashen, S. 1982. *Language Two.* New York: Oxford Press.

Francois, L. 1983. *English in Action: For Adults and Teens. Teacher's Manual--Part 1.* Pre-Publication Edition: Write L.F., 6166 McKinley Ave., South Gate, California 90280.

Galyean, B. 1976. *Language from Within.* Santa Barbara, CA: Confluent Education Development and Research Center.

Garcia, R. 1988. *Instructor's Notebook: How to Apply TPR for Best Results* (Triple Expanded 2nd Edition). Los Gatos, California: Sky Oaks Productions.

Gardner, R. and W. Lambert. 1972. *Attitudes and Motivation in Second Language Learning.* Rowley, Massaachusetts: Newbury House.

Grittner, F. 1977. *Teaching Foreign Languages.* New York: Harper and Row.

Krashen, S. 1982. *Principles and Practice in Second Language Acquisition,* New York: Pergamon Press.

Krashen, S. and Terrell, T. 1983. *The Natural Approach,* Alemany Press, P.O. Box 5265, San Francisco, CA 94101.

Merritt, S. 1987. *Successful, Non-Stressful Learning: A Guide to Accelerated Language Learning.* Merritt Learning Systems, San Diego, California, 92103.

Maculaitis, J. and Scheraga, M. 1981. *What to Do Before the Books Arrive. (And After),* San Francisco: Alemany Press.

Pimsleur, P. and Quinn, T, eds., 1971. *The Psychology of Second Language Learning,* Cambridge: University Press.

Rittenberg, M. and Kreitzer, P. 1981. *English Through Drama,* San Francisco: Alemany Press.

Romijn, E. and Seely, C. 1979. *Live Action English.* San Francisco: Alemany Press.

Savignon, S. 1972. *Communicative Competence: An Experiment in Foreign Language Teaching.* Philadelphia, Pennsylvania: The Center for Curriculum Development.

Segal, B. 1980. *Teaching English Through Action.* 1749 Eucalyptus Street, Brea, CA 92621.

Segal, B. 1981. *Deutschunterricht durch Handeln.* 1749 Eucalyptus Street, Brea, CA 92621.

Segal, B. 1981. *L'Enseignement Du Francais au Moyen de L'Action.* 1749 Eucalyptus Street, Brea, CA 92621.

Segal, B. 1981. *Ensenando El Espanol por Medio de Accion.* 1749 Eucalyptus Street, Brea, CA 92621.

Stevick, Earl W. 1980. *Teaching Languages. A Way and Ways,* Newbury House, Rowley, MA 01969.

Stevick, Earl W. 1976. *Memory, Meaning and Method.* Rowley, Massachusetts: Newbury House.

Terrell, T. "A Natural Approach to the Acquisition and Learning of a Language." *Modern Language Journal* 61: 325-36.

Terrell, T. "The Natural Approach to Language Teaching: An Update." *Modern Language Journal* 66: 121-131.

Reading on Topics of General Relevance

Assagioli, R. 1965. *Psychosynthesis,* New York: Viking.

Assagioli, R. 1973. *The Act of Will,* Baltimore, Maryland: Penguin.

Bandler, R. and Grinder, J. 1981. *Reframing,* Moab, Utah: Real People Press. (On NLP)

Bandler, R. and Grinder, J. *Frogs into Princes,* Real People Press, Box F, Moab, Utah 84532. (On Neuro-Linguistic Programming)

Bandler, R. and Grinder, J. 1975. *Patterns of Hypnotic Techniques of Milton H. Erickson, MD.* Cupertino, California: Meta Publications.

Bandler, R. and Grinder, J. 1975. *The Structure of Magic,* Palo Alto, California: Science and Behavior Books.

Benson, H. 1976. *The Relaxation Response,* New York: Morrow.

Brown, G. 1971. *Human Teaching for Human Learning: An Introduction to Confluent Education,* Viking Press.

Bry, A. 1976. *Visualization: Directing the Movies of Your Mind,* Barnes and Noble.

Canfield, J. and Wells, H. 1976. *100 Ways to Enhance Self-Concept in the Classroom.* Englewood, Cliffs, NJ: Prentice-Hall.

Canfield, J. and Klimek, P. 1978. "Education in the New Age." *New Age Magazine,* February.

Coue, Emile. 1974. *Suggestion and Autosuggestion,* New York: Weiser.

Crampton, M. 1969. "The Use of Mental Imagery in Psychosynthesis." *Journal of Humanistic Psychology* 9:2, pp. 139-153.

De Mille, R. 1973. Put Your Mother on the Ceiling: Children's Imagination Games, Viking Press.

Ferguson, M. 1980. *The Aquarian Conspiracy: Personal and Social Transformation in the 1980's,* J.P. Tarcher.

Ferrucci, P. 1981. *What We May Be: Techniques For Psychological And Spiritual Growth.* Los Angeles: J.P. Tarcher.

Galyean, B. 1983). *Mind Sight.* Long Beach, CA: Center for Integrative Learning.

Gordon, D. 1978. *Therapeutic Metaphors,* Cupertino, California: Meta Publications.

Gordon, D. and Anderson, M. 1982. *Phoenix. Therapeutic Patterns of Milton H. Erickson.*

Gordon, W. G. G. 1961. *Synectics.,* New York: Harper and Row.

Grinder, J. and R. Bandler. 1981. *Tranceformations,* Moab, Utah: Real People Press. (On NLP)

Hall, E. 1959. *The Silent Language.* Greenwich: Fawcett.

Hendricks, G. and Roberts, T. 1977. *The Second Centering Book: More Awareness Activities for Children, Parents, and Teachers.* Englewood Cliffs, New Jersey: Prentice-Hall, Spectrum Books.

Hendricks, G. and Fadiman, J., eds. 1976. *Transpersonal Education: A Curriculum for Feeling and Being.* Englewood Cliffs: Prentice-Hall.

Hendricks, G. and Wills, R. 1975. *The Centering Book: Awareness Activities for Children, Parents, and Teachers.* Englewood Cliffs, New Jersey: Prentice-Hall, Spectrum Books.

Jung, C.G. 1964. *Man and His Symbols.* Garden City, N.Y.: Doubleday.

Koestler, A. 1964. *The Act of Creation,* New York: Macmillan.

Lankton, S. 1980. *Practical Magic,* Meta Publications, Box 565, Cupertino, CA 95014. (On Neuro-Linguistic Programming)

Lee, J. and Pulvino, C. 1978. *Educating the Forgotten Half: Structured Activities for Learning,* Kendall-Hunt Publishers.

Leonard, G. 1968. *Education and Ecstasy,* Delta.

Maslow, A. 1968. *Toward a Psychology of Being.* (2nd ed.). New York: Von Nostrand Reinhold.

Masters, R. and Houston, J. 1973. *Mind Games: the Guide to Inner Space.* New York: Delta/Dell.

May, R. 1975. *The Courage to Create.* New York: Norton.

Moskowitz, G. *Caring and Sharing in the Foreign Language Class,* Newbury House, Rowley, MA 01964.

Ornstein, R. 1973. *The Nature of Human Consciousness,* San Francisco: Freeman and Company Publishers.

Ornstein, R. 1972. *The Psychology of Consciousness,* San Francisco: Freeman and Company Publishers.

Ostrander, S. and Schroeder, L. 1973. *Psychic Discoveries Behind the Iron Curtain.* New York: Bantam Books.

Pelletier, K. 1976. *Mind as Healer. Mind as Slayer,* New York: Delacorte.

Richardson, G. 1983. *Educational Imagery,* Springfield, Illinois: Charles Thomas Publishers.

Roberts, T.B. and Clark, F. 1975. *Transpersonal Psychology in Education.* Bloomington, Indiana: Phi Delta Kappa Educational Foundation, Fastback Pamphlet Series No. 53.

Rossi, E.L. 1980. *The Collected Papers of Milton H. Erickson on Hypnosis.* New York: Irvington Press.

Rozman, D. 1977. *Meditation for Children,* New York: Pocketbooks.

Samples, B. 1976. *The Metaphoric Mind: A Celebration of Creative Consciousness.* Reading, MA: Addison-Wesley.

Samuels, M. and Samuels. N. 1975. *Seeing with the Mind's Eye,* Random House/Bookworks.

ABOUT THE AUTHOR

Lynn Dhority received his Ph.D. from Harvard University, where he was awarded the Boylston Prize for Outstanding Teaching. He is currently a professor of language, literature, and critical and creative thinking at the University of Massachusetts in Boston, where he received the award for Superior Merit in Teaching. His extensive background includes psychology and counseling skills, especially in Psychosynthesis and Neuro-Linguistic Programming (NLP). He was personally trained by Dr. George Lozanov in the art of suggestive-accelerative teaching (Suggestopedia) and has become nationally known as one of the leading teachers and teacher-trainers in holistic education.